The Greatest Guide to
Creative Crafting

This is a **GREATEST**GUIDES title

Greatest Guides Limited, Woodstock, Bridge End, Warwick CV34 6PD, United Kingdom

www.greatestguides.com

Series created by Harshad Kotecha

Greatest Guides is committed to a sustainable future for our planet. This book is printed on paper certified by the Forest Stewardship Council.

MIX
Paper
FSC FSC® C020837

Printed and bound in the United Kingdom

ISBN 978-1-907906-03-9

I would like to thank the following people for their invaluable help in proofreading and for their support:

Jon, my long suffering fiancé

My Mum for her hints, tips and crafting knowledge

Elaine, Sue and Kerry (my 'old' ladies) for their web searching skills and their friendship

Contents

A few words from Lynne …

I have crafted for as long as I can remember, dabbling in
a little bit of everything (sewing, cross stitch, pottery, print
making, card making, glass painting, weaving, bead work,
jewelry making, photography, crochet and knitting to
name just a few). In fact one of my first projects appeared
in Twinkle (a picture paper especially for little girls) at the
ripe old age of four years and ten months. Although to be
honest I think my mum may have done the majority of it. It
consisted of two goldfish in a fish bowl with buttons for the
eyes and bubbles, the brief being to include buttons in the
image you created. So I don't really remember a time when I
haven't made things.

I've had a range of jobs from usherette at the local cinema,
shiner of cutlery at the local airport (for the first class
passengers) to wardrobe mistress at the local theatre (a job
I just loved). However it wasn't until I started to teach adults
at the local college that I found my place in life. It was a
revelation! I could make, craft, talk and get paid for it. My
students became my friends. I was not only the teacher
but also the student, as my students would share their
knowledge with me and I with them. So over the years I've
collected a huge range of hints and tips, many of which are
now within the pages of this book.

It was a difficult task to decide which crafts to include, there
are just so many to choose from. I therefore chose seven
of the most popular (as far as my research showed) those

being: paper crafts, sewing, wool crafts, cross stitch and embroidery, jewelry and bead work, candle making and glass painting.

To build on the tips and tricks I had already collected I 'raided' books and the internet plus crafting family and friends for their top tips. So many tips were willingly 'handed over', that I could have written two books. However only those that made me think 'Well isn't that a clever idea?' were included. I hope these tips will:

- Get you crafting like a professional

- Cut your costs

- Increase your enjoyment

So if you love to craft, want to improve your crafting and save yourself a little money and time into the bargain, this book is for you.

Hope you enjoy.

Lynne

Paper Crafts

" Paper crafting fills my days, not to mention the bedroom, the closet and the living room! **"**

Chapter 1
Paper Crafts

Paper crafts are the ideal way of showing someone how much you care for them and are a great way of keeping your memories alive. Each year thousands of pounds, dollars, yen, euros and francs etc. etc. are spent on paper, card and the many, many tools that can be used to craft cute cards, great gift boxes and super scrapbook pages.

The tips that follow will hopefully improve your paper crafting projects and also save you a little money along the way.

Under pressure

When pressure embossing through a stencil try using some low tack tape to prevent the stencil from moving around as you work. Or if the embossing tool keeps sticking try allowing the paper to warm for a while on the light box before you begin. The heat will soften the fibers of the paper or card and you'll find it easier to emboss.

See the light

When pressure embossing, using a light box makes the process easier. However if you don't have a light box then a good alternative is to use a closed window. Of course it still has to be daylight outside for this to work! Use some low tack tape to help attach everything to the glass.

Under more pressure

You will often find thick paper can tear during embossing. Use the largest balled embossing tool you have and push gently, going over the design a couple of times rather than pushing heavily and going over only once.

Adapting the design of a stencil

When using a stencil to create a craft project, one advantage is you do not have to use the whole design. You can, if you wish, leave part of the design out. If you are making a number of cards and are leaving out the same section of a stencil on all of them, then use masking tape to cover the part you are not using. Then you will not make the mistake and include the section you wish to leave out.

Letter of the law

There is nothing worse than embossing a design only to find when you turn the design over that your letters are the wrong way round. So remember to turn your stencil so the letters read the wrong way round during the embossing process. However it's not all doom and gloom. If you do make a little mistake simply stick the embossed card so the embossing goes 'into' the card rather than sticks out. Who said embossing had to be raised? This sunken effect is called 'de-bossing'.

Brad's not the Pitts!

Want to hide the backs of your brads? Simply line the card you've made with a piece of matching or toning paper. This also works for eyelets. When lining your card remember to trim the lining paper by an eighth of an inch (a couple of centimeters) before inserting. That way you won't have the lining paper peeking out.

Card scoring

To gain a professional look to your cards and boxes always score them before you fold. Simply place a rule where the score is required then run an embossing tool or the nib of a biro that has run out of ink along the rule. One neatly folded project!

Stuck for a solution?

When using mulberry paper or any other handmade paper, many types of glue can show through, spoiling your finish. Use bradlets or eyelets to hold in place for a decorative alternative. Or why not sew in place using a button and some decorative thread? Simply pierce the paper or card with a needle and knot the button in place. This will allow the knot to become a part of the decoration.

Fiddly fibers

With their long fibers mulberry paper and other handmade papers can be very difficult to tear. The solution to this problem is simple! Dampen a fine artists brush and 'draw' a line, then tear along this line whilst still damp. If you wish to create a straighter finish then place a ruler along the dampened line and use this as a guide.

Fiddly process

When using peel-off stickers it is sometimes a fiddly process. The trick is to remove the surrounding area and take a piece of sticky tape and stick it to your hand (to remove some of sticky). Place the tape over the peel-off sticker then pull up the tape taking the peel-off sticker with it. Place the peel-off sticker where it is required on your project then press firmly over the peel-off sticker. Now slowly remove the sticky tape.

All change

Why not try changing your peel-off stickers? By using a small pair of scissors or a sharp craft knife, sections of peel-off stickers can be removed so you can alter the design. Or why not combine different peel-off stickers to change the design?

Create a bunch full

Have a single rose stamp and want to make a bouquet? Then create a mask using a sticky note. Firstly stamp your design near the top of the sticky note, so the adhesive holds the mask in place whilst you work. Cut out the mask then stamp your design onto your paper. Place the mask you created from the sticky note over the image stamped on the paper then stamp again, overlapping your design. In this way half the second stamped image will be on the paper and the other half on the mask. When you remove the mask you have two overlapping images, one appearing behind the other.

Halo effect

If you are using a stamp that has only a little outline detail, with the masking technique try to cut the mask slightly smaller than the stamped image. In this way you'll cut down on the halo effect.

Save yourself time

Masking is a great technique but can be time consuming. So if you know you'll be doing a lot of this, keep the masks you make by sticking them to a page in a folder. That way you'll be able to use them time and time again, saving yourself time when you next craft.

Going around in circles

Improve the finish of your quilling projects by tearing the end that is to be glued. It will stick better and the join will be less visible when the glue has dried. Also, when working with loose coils try to ensure the section pinched contains the join, in this way the join will become hidden.

Flower power

If you're making fringed flowers save time by placing three or four pieces of paper together and cut them at the same time. If when cutting lengths for fringed flowers you're worried you'll cut too far, place the paper into a bulldog clip. Simply place 1/8" (2-3mm) of the paper in the jaws and cut up to the bulldog clip. This will obviously stop you from going any further and cutting the paper in half.

CRAFTY FACT

Rubber stamping as a hobby didn't take off until the 1970s when such companies as All Night Media (in 1974) and Hero Arts (also in 1974) who started to sell these humble craft products.

Make your own backing paper

Bubble painting is the most fun you can have with a straw! Pour water and dishwashing liquid (ratio 50:50) into a shallow bowl, just 1" (2.5cm) deep is all you'll need. Add some color, this could be water colors, out-of-date food dyes, colored ink. Now grab yourself a drinking straw, put one end into the colored water and blow bubbles (remembering not to suck or you'll get a mouthful of dishwashing liquid). When you have a large mound of bubbles take some paper and lower onto the bubbles. Lower the paper until all the bubbles are burst but avoid touching the side of the bowl. Then allow your paper to dry naturally. You can build up colors by bubble painting two or more colors on top of one another. Simply remember to let each color dry completely between layers. Quick, simple and cheap!

Lost your marbles?

Another great way to make your own designer backing paper is marble painting. Simply get a tray, a little paint and some marbles. Place the paper in the base of the tray, and put a little paint in the corner of the tray. Roll the marbles through the paint then over the paper by slightly tipping the tray. If you don't have a tray then use an empty cereal packet. Simply stick down both ends and cut out one large side.

CRAFTY FACT

Paper rolling, paper scrolling and paper filigree are all names paper quilling has also been known by.

Think ink

Don't have a paint the right color but you do have an ink pad? Then use that to paint your images instead. Simply dampen a fine artist's brush, pick up the color on the tip of the brush and paint away.

Chalk alternatives

Do you have an old eye shadow? Then use that rather than investing in new craft chalks. So chalks or eye shadow do not rub off they should be fixed with a fixing spray. If you don't have a fixing spray use cheap hairspray instead, it works just as well. If you don't have any chalk applicators then a good substitute is a cotton wool ball or the make-up brushes used for eye shadow.

Double-sided sticky tape

Looking for a cheap option for your double-sided sticky tape? Then look in your local hardware store for some carpet tape. It's far cheaper and tends to come in much longer lengths. You'll just need to cut it down to use for your crafting.

Make your own embossing powder

Have a few pots of embossing powder with tiny amounts of powder in? Don't let it go to waste, mix them up and see what you get! Keep a record so if you come up with a fantastic new color you can go out and buy some pots of the powders you mixed and make up some more.

All that glitters

Don't have a glitter glue just the right shade? Then make your own using a little clear drying craft glue and some fine glitter. Place in a small syringe, obtainable from most drug stores, and away you go. To store, squirt the glue into an old film canister then press the lid firmly in place and remember to wash out the syringe ready for next time.

Pressure embossing on the dark side

If you're pressure embossing onto dark card or paper and cannot see through it then don't give up. Gently rub the bowl of a spoon over the paper or card with the stencil in position to start you off. This will give you a faint outline to work with, making life much easier.

Stenciling with color

When adding color through stencils start with the lightest color first, using a sponge. This will cut down on the amount of cleaning you will have to do on the sponge you are using and won't 'muddy' the colors.

Buttons

Need to remove the shank from a button for a project? Use a pair of old nail clippers. They're safe, easy to use and inexpensive.

CRAFTY FACT

Did you know that up until 1770 bread crumbs were used to remove pencil marks? Sir Joseph Priestly is the man we can thank for his comments on the properties of rubber and its ability to remove pencil marks.

" Paper crafting forever, household chores... whenever! **"**

Double-sided sticky pads

Removing the backing paper from a double-sided pad can sometimes be frustrating. To make the removal easier press in the middle of the pad with an embossing tool or pair of tweezers; the edges of the backing paper will lift slightly allowing you to peel the backing off with ease.

Embossing heat

It is easy to burn your fingers when heat embossing small items. So in order to avoid this, hold the item in a clothespin or small, clean pair of long-nosed pliers so that fingers are kept out of the way. Alternatively place on a heat resistant surface and hold in place with a pencil.

Make it quick

If you place a piece of foil under the card whilst you heat emboss it will help speed up the embossing process, as the metal foil will reflect the heat.

Don't get stuck with static

If static is a problem on your paper crafting projects then you can purchase anti-static bags. However you could try sprinkling a little baby powder on the surface of your paper or card. Tap off excess powder then stamp or wipe over the surface with a tumble dryer sheet prior to stamping.

Is it done yet?

If you are not sure if your embossing powder has fully melted, stop. Hold the project up to the light to check. If only some of the powder has melted, heat again. It does not harm the embossing powder if you stop halfway through the heating process. However it is possible to overheat embossing powder so care has to be taken.

Punch power

Don't forget when you punch out a section of card or paper you also have the little sections you punched out. These can be used to decorate a range of paper craft projects too, so nothing is wasted. For example these small shapes are ideal for making shaker cards.

Stick with it

Should you want some small simple decorations then why not use your punches with some paper that is pre-glued on the reverse? Simply punch as normal and your shapes will be already sticky, saving time and fuss later.

CRAFTY FACT

It was not until cheap paper was invented that 'working class' women were able to enjoy the art of paper quilling. During the Stuart, Georgian and Regency periods quilling was only enjoyed by ladies of the aristocracy. The reason being that these ladies were the only people who had the time to spare and could afford to craft with such a luxury item.

Tearing along

If you are tearing paper for a project and don't want a white line around the torn section then tear from the back. If you want a particular shape, cut the shape needed from thick card then use this as a cheap tearing tool. Place it on the back of the paper then tear the paper up against the edges of the card. In this way you'll be able to tear the same shape time and time again.

Picture perfect

When creating pages with original photographs do ensure you use acid free products to ensure a long life to your design. This is also true of all the other materials you use, including glue. Today many types of glue are specially designed for use in scrapbooking, so remember to read the labels to make sure they are pH neutral.

"The purpose of crafting is to stop time."

Keeping 'em clean

Want to keep your wood mounted rubber stamps looking like new? Simply cover the wooden part of the rubber stamp with clear nail polish. Allow it to fully dry and when you clean your stamp after use the ink will come off with ease.

CRAFTY FACT

In June 1844 Charles Goodyear patented his method for turning basic rubber into something that could be used for a million and one uses. So rubber stampers rejoice at the hours spent by Mr. Goodyear experimenting. If it were not for him and his efforts we would not have the humble rubber stamp.

Make it personal

Why not personalize your projects by using the relevant Zodiac sign, flower or stone associated with the recipient's birthday?

Dates	Sign	Symbol	Flower	Stone
22nd December to 19th January	Capricorn	Sea Goat	Pansy	Garnet
20th January to 18th February	Aquarius	Water Bearer	Golden Rod or Orchid	Amethyst
19th February to 20th March	Pisces	Fish	Water-lily	Aquamarine
21st March to 19th April	Aries	Ram	Honeysuckle or Daisy	Diamond
20th April to 20th May	Taurus	Bull	Rose or Poppy	Emerald
21st May to 21st June	Gemini	Twins	Lily-of-the-Valley	Pearl

Dates	Sign	Symbol	Flower	Stone
22nd June to 22nd July	Cancer	Crab	Acanthus	Ruby
23rd July to 22nd August	Leo	Lion	Marigold or Sunflower	Peridot
23rd August to 22nd September	Virgo	Virgin	Anemone	Sapphire
23rd September to 22nd October	Libra	Scales	Hydrangea	Opal
23rd October to 21st November	Scorpio	Scorpion	Geranium	Topaz
22nd November to 21st December	Sagittarius	Archer	Carnation	Turquoise

Or go Celtic

Alternatively you could use the following Celtic animals, stone or planet symbols as your inspiration.

Dates	Animal	Tree	Stone	Planet
24th December to 20th January	Stag	Birch	Crystal	The Sun
21st January to 17th February	Crane	Rowan	Peridot	Uranus
18th February to 17th March	Seal	Ash	Coral	Neptune
18th March to 14th April	Bear	Alder	Ruby	Mars

Dates	Animal	Tree	Stone	Planet
15th April to 12th May	Adder	Willow	Moonstone	Moon
13th May to 9th June	Bee	Hawthorn	Topaz	Vulcan
10th June to 7th July	Otter	Oak	Diamond	Jupiter
8th July to 4th August	Cat	Holly	Red Carnelian	Earth
5th August to 1st September	Salmon	Hazel	Amethyst	Mercury
2nd September to 29th September	Swan	Grape Vine	Emerald	Venus
30th September to 27th October	Goose	Ivy	Opal	Moon
28th October to 24th November	Owl	Reed	Jasper	Pluto
25th November to 23rd December	Raven	Elder	Jet	Saturn

Or why not go Oriental and use the Chinese Zodiac based on the birth year?

It could be original and appropriate to use birth signs from the Chinese Zodiac. Legend has it the 12 animals of the Chinese Zodiac were chosen by Buddha. When Buddha was near death he invited all the animals to visit him. Only 12 came: the rat, ox, tiger, rabbit, dragon, snake, horse, goat, monkey, rooster, dog and pig. For visiting him, Buddha honoured each by using them to represent the 12 phases of the Zodiac.

Rat

| 1900 | 1912 | 1924 | 1936 | 1948 | 1960 | 1972 | 1984 | 1996 | 2008 |

Ox

| 1901 | 1913 | 1925 | 1937 | 1949 | 1961 | 1973 | 1985 | 1997 | 2009 |

Tiger

| 1902 | 1914 | 1926 | 1938 | 1950 | 1962 | 1974 | 1986 | 1998 | 2010 |

Rabbit

| 1903 | 1915 | 1927 | 1939 | 1951 | 1963 | 1975 | 1987 | 1999 | 2011 |

Dragon

| 1904 | 1916 | 1928 | 1940 | 1952 | 1964 | 1976 | 1988 | 2000 | 2012 |

Snake

| 1905 | 1917 | 1929 | 1941 | 1953 | 1965 | 1977 | 1989 | 2001 | 2013 |

Horse

| 1906 | 1918 | 1930 | 1942 | 1954 | 1966 | 1978 | 1990 | 2002 | 2014 |

Goat

| 1907 | 1919 | 1931 | 1943 | 1955 | 1967 | 1979 | 1991 | 2003 | 2015 |

Monkey

| 1908 | 1920 | 1932 | 1944 | 1956 | 1968 | 1980 | 1992 | 2004 | 2016 |

Rooster

| 1909 | 1921 | 1933 | 1945 | 1957 | 1969 | 1981 | 1993 | 2005 | 2017 |

Dog

| 1910 | 1922 | 1934 | 1946 | 1958 | 1970 | 1982 | 1994 | 2006 | 2018 |

Pig

| 1911 | 1923 | 1935 | 1947 | 1959 | 1971 | 1983 | 1995 | 2007 | 2019 |

Sewing

" Just like Madonna I'm a material girl. Do you wanna see my fabric collection? "

Chapter 2
Sewing

Throughout history the art of sewing has been vital for clothing the family and making items for the home. However in recent years the ability to sew has not been necessary as clothing is now relatively cheap. Today sewing has become a pastime that allows the sewer to create individual items for the home and items to wear, rather than a necessary chore. Unfortunately, because sewing is no longer passed from one generation to the next many of the old tricks have almost been forgotten. So read on and hopefully the tips included will improve your sewing and save you both time and money.

Create your own index

Does your machine have a whole range of programmed stitches on it? Do you actually know what all these stitches look like? If not then why not stitch your decorative stitches onto a piece of fabric, then write beneath each one what they are. In this way when you work on your next sewing project you can simply and easily choose a stitch that is just right.

CRAFTY FACT

Many Victorian thimbles were made of silver and during the First World War they were collected and melted down to buy hospital equipment.

It's this wide

Many new machines have markings on the foot plate which are 1/8" (0.5cm), 3/8" (1cm) and 5/8" (1.5cm) from the needle, when it is in the middle position. However if you are using an old machine these markings may not be there. So use a little masking tape instead. Simply run the edge of your fabric along the edge of the tape for the perfect seam width every time. Just remember to keep your needle in the same position, otherwise you'll alter the width the needle is away from the masking tape.

Cutting it

For accurate cutting, always leave the lower blade of your scissors on the cutting table. If you raise the blade as you cut you create edges that look like the hamster has been at them!

Magnetic charm

Keep dropping those pins and needles and find it difficult to pick them up? Then find yourself a magnet. If you have difficulty bending down, then simply hang your magnet on a piece of thread. Also next time you go to throw out an old bag or purse with a magnetic clasp 'rescue' the magnet before you throw it out.

CRAFTY FACT

Know what a digitabulist is? Well it's a person who collects thimbles.

Pinned down

If you find it difficult to pin heavy fabrics then try pushing the pins into a bar of soap before you start your project. It will allow the pins to slip into the fabric easier, grip the fabric better and the added bonus is it will wash out when laundered, leaving no marks behind.

Sheer delight

When pinning sometimes the pins can leave marks in the fabric, especially when working on very thin, delicate or heavyweight rigid fabrics. To avoid this, pin inside the seam allowance. This way when you sew, any pin marks created will disappear inside the seam.

Soft soap

On holiday or away from all your usual little tools and keep losing your pins? That bar of soap comes to the rescue again – this time as a pin cushion.

Pressing engagement

To add that professional touch when sewing make sure you press at every stage. And if you are working with a fabric that could easily mark, use a pressing cloth, damp if possible, for perfect results every time.

Fun with fur

When sewing with fur, the pile often gets stuck in the seaming. To hide the seaming simply take a needle with a blunt end and rub it back and forth over the seam. This will lift the pile out of the seam and it'll almost disappear.

Which way up

When working with fur, remember that the pile has an up and a down, which is important to get in the right direction (the pile should run down). So, before you start to cut out, draw arrows on the back of the fabric telling you the direction of the fur. This will ensure you don't make a mistake when you are laying out your pattern.

Make it safe

When making toys ensure you use safety features and fillings that are suitable for toys and that the filling meets the fire and safety standard regulations.

Perfect hem

Different fabrics react differently and some are prone to stretching (especially when cut on the cross, 45°). So always allow a garment to hang for a day or so in a warm room to allow it to drop. This will help you create a hem that is straight every time.

Salvage that selvage

When making up a project never use the selvage (the tightly woven section of the fabric on the very edge). When washed this section of the fabric reacts differently to the rest and can often shrink, causing puckering on that new garment you've spent an age making.

Bothersome buttons

When cutting a buttonhole it is easy to cut too far. To avoid this, place a pin at either end of the buttonhole, just inside the stitching. The pins then stop you cutting too far. Also rather than using a small pair of scissors for this delicate job use a good quality stitch ripper. Mixed with the pin tip above you'll have perfect buttonholes every time.

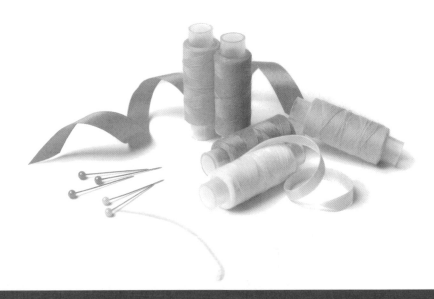

" You know I'd rather be stitching than in the kitchen! **"**

Cheap to expensive

If you are working with a cheap fabric and have plenty of it why not have a double layer? It will make the end result look a million dollars!

Tack away

Tacking can be a boring task, however (along with pressing between each stage) tacking can improve the finished garment no end. The secret of the perfect zip is tacking, the secret to the ultimate dart is tacking and the secret to the perfectly fitted sleeve is – yes, you've got it – tacking!

Hang with it

Have you completed a garment that keeps falling off the hanger and needs hanging straps? The problem with hanging straps is they often peek out during wear. To overcome this problem simply attach them using snap fasteners (press studs). Sew one half of the snap fastener to the shoulder seam and the other half to the hanging strap. That way you can take them off during wear and put them back on when needed.

Craftsmen and their tools

We all know that lint accumulates in and around the bobbin case of a sewing machine. Rather than blowing this lint to remove it, use the fine hose on your vacuum cleaner. Once you've done this, place a little machine oil onto a clean piece of rag and wipe over any moving parts (all this should be done with the machine unplugged for safety). This should ensure your machine is kept in 'perfect health.'

Fantastic elastic

When you need to attach a row of equally spaced buttons, buttonholes, snaps or hooks and eyes, grab a piece of elastic. Mark equally spaced points on it; align the first where you want the top button, buttonhole etc. then stretch the elastic the correct length. The marks will move and work out the correct placement. Then simply transfer the markings using a fabric pen.

With care

When you buy a new piece of fabric make a note of the care instructions written on the roll. When at home tack these instructions to the fabric. When you come to make your project, place these instructions in a little book, along with a small sample of the fabric. You then have a record of how to care for the project when complete. If the fabric you have chosen has care instructions on the selvage then simply cut this off, zigzag or overlock the edges and make yourself a small care label, which can be sewn into one of the seams.

All zipped up

To cut down on frustration always check a zip works properly before fitting it in your project.

Chalked out

Next time you stay in a hotel or B&B pick up that tiny bar of soap at the end of your stay. Then when you get home you can use it instead of chalk. It creates a soft fine line on many medium to dark fabrics and will wash out during the first wash.

Basic sewing kit

Whether you do a lot of sewing or not, every home should have a basic sewing and mending kit for those last minute mending chores. Here are the basics and you can expand from there:

- Sewing machine – choose a model with a one-step buttonholer, ability to drop the feed dog, straight stitch in a variety of lengths, zigzag stitch in a variety of widths and the ability to sew backwards and a selection of feet including a zipper foot

- Spools of all-purpose polyester thread, in a range of colors

- Scissors in various sizes

- Small measuring tape or cloth tape

- Packet of assorted multi-use darning needles

- Packet of long straight pins – with large glass or plastic heads

- Packet of safety pins

- Pin cushion

- Seam ripper – the sharp, curved edge is used to cut seams open, while the fine point is used to pick out threads

- Self-fastening tape such as iron-on hem tape

- A thimble – find one that fits your middle finger

- A needle threader, which saves lots of time and frustration

- Snap fasteners (sizes 3/0, 2/0, & 0)

- Hooks & eyes (sizes 1, 2 & 3)

- 6" (15cm) ruler or sewing gauge

- Assortment of patches

- Small jar or container with an assortment of buttons

- Sewing box or small plastic storage container to hold it all

66 Never let your sewing machine know you're in a hurry! **99**

Fit that zip

When fitting a zip don't be tempted to sew down one side, across the bottom then back up the other side. This will pull the fabric down as you machine down and up as you machine up, causing your zip to bend and twist. The secret to sewing in the perfect zip (once you've tacked it in place of course) is to sew down one side, come out and cast off. Then come down the other side and repeat the process. Also remember to use a zipper foot which will allow you to get closer to the zip, giving you a neater finish.

Don't come apart at the seams

A quick and easy way to ensure your seams don't come undone is to securely knot them off then to weave the ends of the thread in and out of the last three or four stitches. However if you are pushed for time then at the beginning of the seam stitch six stitches, reverse for six, then sew the rest of the seam as normal. At the end of the seam repeat by reversing six stitches then go forward again. In this way you'll have a dozen stitches that will have to come undone before your seam starts to unravel.

Measured out

If you have to lengthen a pattern piece, rather than using plain drafting paper use 'dot and cross' or paper that has a grid on it. This will allow you to open out the section you need evenly across the whole pattern without having to fuss with a ruler.

Perfect pockets

When creating patch pockets on a garment made from patterned fabric, the ultimate in finish is to match the pattern on the garment and the pocket. To do this, first cut out the section that will have the pocket on and tailor tack the position of the pocket. Place the tissue pattern of the pocket in place. Then using a disappearing marker (just in case you go through the tissue paper) trace off the most important/main sections of the pattern. When you place the pocket pattern on the fabric, match the design drawn on the pattern with the design on the fabric beneath. This will give you a pocket that once sewn in place will simply blend into the garment.

Thread horror

Ever finished sewing and you look down and your carpet is littered with hundreds of threads that simply refuse to go up the vacuum cleaner? Fear not. Grab a tumble drier sheet, roll it into a ball and rub over the offending cottons; they'll stick to it like glue.

CRAFTY FACT

Native Americans used a plant called the agave plant which provided not just the needle but the thread also. The leaf was soaked over a long period of time in water. This left a pulp made up of long stringy fibers with a sharp tip. The sharp tip came from the tip of the leaf. It was this that was used to sew skins and clothes together.

On the move

Many a sewer will want to take a little project with them whilst they're away. With today's travel restrictions on many, if not all, airlines you are unable to take scissors in your hand luggage. A great way to overcome this is to take an empty dental floss box with you. The little 'cutter' used to cut the floss can be used to cut your threads instead.

The big time

When working on a large project you just know one bobbin isn't going to be enough. So fill two or three bobbins at the same time and place to one side for use later. When your bobbin runs out you'll have one ready to go. Bliss!

The big shrink

Using a fabric you have never used before? Before you start do a small test to see if it shrinks. To do this measure a square of fabric, wash it and then re-measure once dry. If you find the piece has shrunk then you'll know you'll have to wash the whole piece of fabric before making up your project.

Naughty thread

Sometimes when threading a needle the thread will just not do as it's told. To make life a little easier cut the end of the thread at 45°. In this way the thread is easier to get through the eye. Also try placing a sheet of white paper behind the needle; this should help your aim.

Wrinkle free

Before you lay a pattern onto the fabric set the iron to cool and with the print side down give the pattern a quick iron. In this way you'll remove any folds or wrinkles in the pattern making pinning easier.

Testers

Don't throw away the scraps of fabric left over; keep them close to hand in a container. Then when you start your project you can use them to ensure your machine is sewing correctly. In the trade this collection of remnant fabric scraps is known as the 'cabbage patch'.

All change

When working on a sewing machine ideally you should change the needle you are working with after six to ten hours of sewing use. This will cut down on the possibility of the needle becoming blunt and the chance of the needle breaking whilst you are sewing.

CRAFTY FACT

Thimbles have not always been used just as a sewing aid. During the 1800s they were used to measure spirits, hence the phrase 'just a thimbleful.' They were also used by 'ladies' of the night, who would wear them and tap on a window to announce their presence, known as thimble-knocking.

Victorian schoolmistresses would also thimble-knock the heads of pupils if they were too unruly.

Feet firmly on the ground

Most modern sewing machines come with an accessory pack including a few feet. However there is a whole range of feet, so what follows is a list of the basic feet available:

Sewing machine feet

Name	Use
Binding foot	This allows you to apply pre-folded bias binding to raw edges
Blind hem foot	If you're in a hurry and don't want to sew a hem by hand then this foot (if you have it on your machine) will allow you to use the blind hem stitch with ease
Button hole foot	If your machine can produce one-step or four-step buttonhole stitch you can use this foot. Some allow you to place the button in the rear of the foot, so you don't have to measure the hole required, the machine does it for you
Cording foot	This foot has a hole, sometimes two or three, which allows you to place a cord through it then zigzag the cord in place
Darning foot	This is an open circle, oval, square or rectangle with the inside hole varying in size. It is ideal for working with the feed dog in the down position, perhaps when working free-motion embroidery

Name	Use
Embroidery foot	These are usually made from clear plastic so you can see through them. A groove is cut on the underside of the foot so the work is not flattened as you sew
Gathering foot	This foot will gather fabric as you sew. It can be used on a single piece of fabric or will allow you to attach a frill to another in one go
Narrow hemming foot	This rolls the raw edge of fabric as you sew, creating a narrow double rolled hem. Best used with lightweight fabrics
Opened toed foot	This machine foot is very wide and is ideal for keeping an eye on your stitching
Over-casting foot	Will allow you to stitch right on the edge of the fabric. They often have a brush underneath to help stop rolling and puckering as you sew
Pin tuck foot	Use this foot with a twin needle to create quick and simple narrow pin tucks
Teflon coated foot	As the name suggests this is coated with Teflon and is ideal when working on plastic or PVS-coated fabrics
Walking foot	Helps to feed fabrics such a fur as you stitch, improving the finish of your seams
Zigzag foot	This foot is wider than the general all-purpose foot and allows the needle to swing left and right as you sew
Zipper foot	These vary in design and allow you to sew close to the teeth on a zip, giving you a more professional finish

" A yard of fabric is like chocolate cake, you can never have enough. **"**

Sewing machine needles

Needles are given a number to indicate both the length and the thickness. Matching the needle size to your fabric removes the frustration of creating holes in your fabric or the needle continually breaking.

American sizes	European sizes	Suggested suitable fabrics
8	60	Very fine sheer fabrics
9	65	Silks and fine fabrics
10	70	Lightweight fabrics
11	75	Light to medium weight fabrics
12	80	Light to medium weight fabrics
14	90	Medium weight cottons or similar, suitable for most dressmaking projects
16	100	Medium to heavy weight fabrics for example canvas
18	110	Heaving weight fabrics such as heavy curtaining fabric
19	120	Extremely heavy weight fabrics or fabrics with backing

Sewing machine needle types

Name	Uses
Ballpoint needle	Has a rounded tip and is ideal if your fabric keeps on 'snagging' whilst you are sewing, use on knits or fine fabrics

Name	Uses
Denim or Jeans needle	This needle has a very sharp point and a strong shaft so is ideal when working on heavy canvas or denim
Embroidery needle	This needle has a slightly rounded point, a large eye and a deeper groove in the shaft. It is ideal when you are working with decorative threads which are likely to break
Hemstitch/wing needle	Fins or wings on either side of the shank create holes in tightly woven fabrics and are used for decorative stitching
Leather needle	The point is shaped like a wedge which makes a large hole as it goes through the fabric. This allows the home sewer to take on more difficult-to-sew fabrics such as leather or heavy vinyl
Metallic thread needle	The large eye of this needle is coated with Teflon which reduces the friction between the needle and the thread. Ideal when working with delicate metallic or invisible threads
Sharp point needle (Microtex)	This needle is sharper and thinner than the universal needle (see below), is able to pierce layers of fabrics and is ideal for creating button holes
Skip-free needle	This has a deep groove above the eye of the needle and is suitable when using thicker threads to sew with or when working on slightly thicker fabrics
Spring needle	This needle has a wire spring to stop fabrics from riding up when working on a project where the feed dog has been lowered and/or the pressure foot has been removed, for example when free-arm embroidering

Name	Uses
Stretch needle	As the name suggests this needle is suitable for use with fabrics that stretch such as jersey or lycra. It has a specially shaped shank that creates good, even stitches. It can also improve the sewing of your machine when working with fake fur
Topstitching needle	An extra large eye and a deeper than usual groove in the shaft allows the sewer to use heavier threads or even use a double thread if desired
Twin/triple needle	These allow the sewer to create perfectly spaced, parallel rows of stitching
Quilt needle	With its tapered point and stronger shaft this needle is ideal when working through lots of layers such as a quilting project
Universal/general needle	Ideal for general sewing projects and can be used on most medium weight woven and knitted fabrics

Hand sewing needle types

Needle Name	Uses
Ball point	Has a blunted/rounded end which is ideal for sewing on fine fabric or those that are likely to snag
Beading	These are very fine, often long needles that will fit through the center of beads and sequins
Betweens (Quilting)	Have a small rounded eye, used for fine stitches on heavy fabrics or when working with lots of layers
Bodkin	Long, thick needles with a ballpoint end and a large eye, useful for threading elastic or ribbons through casings

Needle Name	Uses
Chenille	Large long eye, sharp point, similar to tapestry needles. Useful for sewing through close weave fabrics
Darning	Have a blunt tip and a large eye and are often available up to size 18
Doll	These are long, thin needles used for creating the features on soft dolls
Embroidery (Crewel)	These are identical to sharps but have a longer eye to make threading easier
Easy/Self-threading	Similar to sharps but have a slot rather than an eye
Leather (Glovers)	These needles have a triangular shaped point for piercing leather without tearing it. Useful not just on leather but also suede, plastics and vinyls
Milliners'	Longer than sharps, useful for pleating and basting
Sailmaker	Similar in shape to leather needles, however the triangular shape extends further up the length of the needle. They are useful for sewing thick fabrics such as heavy canvas
Sharps	Good for general sewing and they have a sharp point
Tapestry	These have a large eye and a blunt tip, used when working on canvas or even-weave fabrics
Tatting	They are long and the same thickness the entire length of the needle
Upholstery	Long, heavy needles, available straight or curved. Used for sewing very heavy fabrics/upholstery projects

Seams easy enough

Using the right seam can make or break a sewing project. So what follows are step-by-step instructions for a range of different seams, all of which are suitable for different projects and fabric types. So you can simply choose the seam you want to match the project you are working on.

Top-stitched

A simple yet effective stitch both useful for adding decoration and extra strength when needed, for example children's clothes.

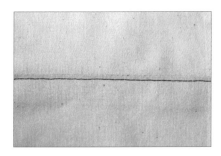

How to sew a top-stitched seam

1. Place fabric right sides together and sew 2/8" (5mm) in from the edge.

2. Press the seam open then finish raw edges in preferred way.

3. Then press the seam to one side.

4. Working on the right side of the fabric sew a second row 1/8" (2mm) away from the first row of stitching, through the pressed seam allowance.

Edge stitched seam

This is useful if you do not have an over-locker or the zig-zag facility on your machine. It can also be useful when working with a light to medium weight fabric which tends to fray badly. Although it is not advisable to use this on a heavy weight fabric as it tends to add bulk to your finished seam.

How to sew an edge stitched seam

1. Place your fabric right sides together and sew 5/8" (1.5cm) in from the edge.

2. Then fold under the raw edges of the seam by 2/8" (5mm) and sew in place close to the folded edge.

3. Press open for a neat finish.

Flat fell seam

This seam is great for adding additional detailing to your project but also has two added benefits. Firstly it lays flat against the body so is ideal for garments such as pajamas and secondly it is very hard wearing so great for kids' clothes.

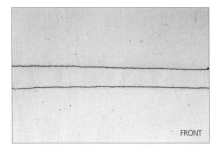
FRONT

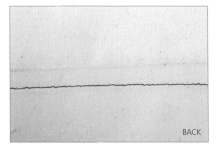
BACK

How to sew a flat fell seam

1. Place your fabric wrong sides together and sew 5/8" (1.5cm) in from the edge.

2. Trim one side of the seam to 2/8" (5mm) of the first line of stitching.

3. On the un-trimmed edge turn the fabric under by 2/8" (5mm).

4. Now press the seam flat and sew 1/8″ (2mm) from the folded edge encasing the trimmed raw edge within the seam.

Notes:

Always work this seam so the seam lies to the back of the body.

If you do not want both lines of stitching to be seen on the outside (right side) of the garment then sew with right sides together in step one.

French seam

The French seam is a neat seam that encases all raw edges within it once complete. It is ideal for very fine fabrics which fray badly and for clothes to be worn by infants and children.

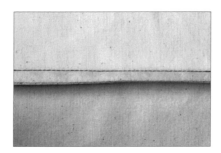

How to sew a French seam

1. Place your fabric wrong sides together and sew 2/8″ (5mm) in from the edge.

2. Press the seam open.

3. Fold seam back on itself so the fabric is now right sides together.

4. Press so the first seam runs along the very edge of the fold.

5. Sew 1/4″ (1cm) from the folded edge to complete.

Under-stitched seam

This seam is used to help the finish of your garment as it reduces the chances of facings poking out during wear.

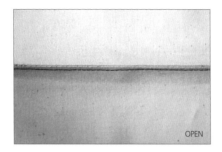
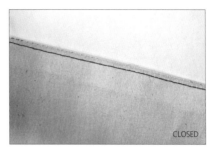

How to sew an under-stitched seam

1. Place fabric and facing right sides together and sew 5/8" (1.5cm) in from the edge.

2. Cut and trim the seam as necessary to allow it to lay flat.

3. Press the seams towards the facing.

4. Position the facing right side up under your sewing machine.

5. Sew the facing to the seam allowance sewing 1/8" (2mm) from the original sewing line, ensuring as you sew that the facing lies flat.

Corded seam

Sewn in a very similar way to the piped seam this method gives a little added depth to your project.

How to sew a corded seam

1. Open out a strip of bias binding which is the same length as your seam and then fold in half.

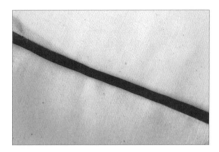

2. Insert the cord, placing it right up to the fold and tack in place using small tacking stitches.

3. On the right side position the bias binding so the original fold lines lay on the seam allowance, 5/8" (1.5cm) in from the edge and tack in place.

4. Place the second piece of fabric on top with right sides together and tack in place.

5. Sew in normal way.

6. Finish raw edges using preferred method.

7. Press seam open being careful not to 'crush' the cord.

Notes:

Pre-covered cord can be purchased if you need to save yourself time.

The secret to getting close to the cord is using a special cording foot or a zipper foot.

Should you wish to leave out the cord then this seam becomes a piped seam.

Strap seam

This is a lovely seam for heavier fabrics and when making unlined coats and jackets.

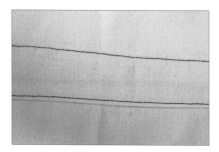

How to sew a strap seam

1. With right sides together sew a 5/8" (1.5cm) seam and press open.

2. Trim edges to 1cm (1/4").

3. Cut a strip of fabric the same length as the seam 5/8" (1.5cm) wide then press under 1/8" (5mm) on either side of the strip.

4. Place the strip centrally over the seam then tack in place.

5. Now sew along the strip close to the folded edges.

Note:

This seam can be used as a decorative feature by simply starting with wrong sides together and attaching the strap to the right side of the garment.

Bound seam

This seam is great for unlined coats and jackets and for using on fabrics that are slightly heavy in weight and which fray easily.

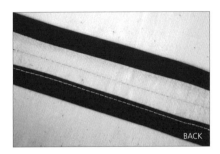

How to sew a bound seam

1. Place your fabric right sides together and sew 2/8" (5mm) in from the edge.

2. Press the seam open.

3. Open out one side of the bias binding and lay so the edge matches the raw edge of one side of the seam on the right side of the fabric.

4. Sew (single layer) using the fold line of the bias binding as your guide.

5. Repeat this for the other side of the seam.

6. Now fold the binding over and around the raw edge and using the machine stitching line hand stitch the bias binding in place.

7. Repeat this for the other side to complete.

Note:

For speed the second row of stitching on the binding can be produced on the machine, however the finish is not as neat as the stitching can be seen.

Hints and tips for perfect seams

Now you know what seam is best for your projects what follows are a few tips that will ensure a high level of finish:

- When pressing if the seam is horizontal then press in a downwards direction. If the seam is vertical then press towards the side of the body.

- By using a contrasting or complementary color thread, seams such as the top stitched seam can be used for decoration.

- Before you make your project using a shop purchased pattern check the amount allowed for seams. Normally it is 5/8" (1.5cm), however there are exceptions to this rule.

- When working with a fabric which frays always neaten the raw edges of your seam, this will prolong the life of your project.

- Pick a color as near to the color of your fabric as possible. If your fabric is patterned then pick a thread that matches the most dominant color.

- If you are working with a heavy weight fabric you may wish to reduce the bulk of the seam by trimming one side of the seam by half. On many patterns this is called 'layering'.

- If you are working on a curved seam, to encourage it to lay flat you may wish to clip into the seam – this is known as 'clipping'. For an inside curve (concaved) simply cut from the edge to as close to the seam as you can without cutting the seam every 1" (2.5cm). If you are working on a curve that is an outside curve (convex) then cut small V's from the edge to as close to the seam as you can without cutting the seam. Then when the seam is turned the V's will close up but will not add bulk to the seam.

Wool Crafts

" For people allergic to wool, one's heart can only bleed. **"**

Chapter 3
Wool Crafts

Knitting, crocheting and weaving have not always been fashionable crafts. However many, many crafters continue to create with wool from the most basic pram covers and baby garments, right up to high fashion garments and chic accessories made from modern luxury yarns. Spurred on by celebrities these highly addictive crafts have found a new audience. After picking many an 'old' brain the tips that follow are sure to help you create some wonderful woolly wotsits!

What size?

Before you begin a new project ensure you're making the right size. Find someone willing to help, hand them a tape measure and get them measuring. Do not use a fabric tape measure as they can stretch over time and give false measurements. Write the measurements down and check them against the finished sizes of your pattern, then adjust as needed.

What should be measured?

Not sure what to measure? The following list should cover all bases: bust or chest, length from back neck, sleeve seam (up to underarm) for sweaters, cardigans and jackets. Waist and hip measurements for skirts plus skirt length (which is personal choice), plus leg length for trousers or baby rompers and diameter of the crown for hats.

Beads galore

Adding beads to your projects can add extra dimension and interest. However beads can rub and cause friction. To cut down on the friction whilst working, wax your wool first. Also ensure the wool you choose is strong and can withstand the extra wear and tear.

Alternate holder

If you're looking for a cheap holder for your crochet hooks then next time you're out and about pick up a toothbrush holder, the type you place your toothbrush in when you're traveling. And at the same time why not treat yourself to a small make-up bag which you can use to hold scissors, needles etc.

Where'd I get to?

Patterns can be expensive, so to protect them whilst you are working place them in a plastic wallet. If you need to make notes or mark where you have got to, then use a Post-it note. Once you have finished place it so that it underlines the line you are on inside the plastic wallet. In this way it should still be in the right place next time you pick up your project to continue. Placing sheets in a wallet in this way allows you to store all your patterns in a folder, which can be divided into types of garments making it easier to locate the pattern you want.

CRAFT FACT
Did you know that there are 50 steps in making a single simple bamboo knitting needle?

Pressing engagement

Once your project is finished and you're ready to sew it together then it is always advisable to block and press each piece first, which will reshape each section and smooth out the stitches. This will not only make the stitches nice and even but should also prevent the edges from rolling, giving you a more professional finish. However the rib rarely needs pressing, so if it is part of one section of your project do not press the rib as this will flatten it, which will then reduce its elasticity.

Music to my ears

When following a pattern or instructions from a book or pamphlet it can sometimes refuse to sit still. To solve the problem why not invest in a music stand or a cook book holder, often available in kitchen stores. These will hold your book or pamphlet open for you and allow you to concentrate on your project.

Stop the rock and roll

As you work, the ball of yarn will be tempted to roll over the floor. The easiest way to stop this is to pull the center of the ball of wool out and work from the middle. However if this is not possible then there are a number of cheap methods you can employ. You could use a plastic bag that has a zip to lock. Snip one of the corners and thread the end of the wool through the hole, then place the wool in the bag, sealing tightly. Or take an empty plastic bottle, cut the bottom off and slip the end of the wool through the hole at the top, stand it upright and begin your project. These methods also give the benefit that the wool stays cleaner and is kept out of the way of playful pets.

In the round

When you are working in the round it can be very difficult to keep a track of what row you're on. To help, place a stitch marker at the beginning of the first row, then when you've worked the first row move the marker up one row. Continue in this way until you've completed your project.

Magic marker

When working on a difficult project you may want to mark a spot, for which you can purchase stitch markers. However there are lots of clever ways to mark your stitch using items that you may already have lying around the house. The small plastic tags off bread bags are ideal or use a small length of bright or different colored wool and loop it through the stitch. Once you've finished you can simply give it a little pull and no one will ever know it was there. Pipe cleaners are also ideal, simply cut to around 1" (2.5cm) long, put through the stitch, bend in half and twist the ends. When you've completed simply untwist and remove. The added bonus here is they can be used many times before they become 'tired.'

On the edge

If you find your cast-on edge is too tight try casting on with a pair of needles that are a size larger than the size you'll be using for the rest of the project. When you have finished casting on change to the correct size needles and your tension should be much improved.

Oh those ends

Don't know what to do with your ends? Simply thread the ends into a large eyed needle and weave through the back of the stitches. If you travel through half a dozen or so in one direction then work back in the other, this should ensure the ends don't work loose during wear.

A knotty problem

Sometimes you'll be working and find a large knot in the middle of your ball of wool. Resist the temptation to work the knot in, rather unpick to the beginning of the row, cut the knot out then rejoin. If you don't resist the temptation it's quite likely the knot could work its way through to the right side of the project and be seen during wear.

Stop frustration

When purchasing your wool ensure you buy enough to finish not just the making but also the sewing of your project. This not only saves you the trip to buy extra but the frustration when you find you are unable to get hold of the same color batch.

Band aid

When you buy wool the balls often come with bands around the middle. These tend to contain lots of useful information. For example what the wool is made from (is it pure wool, a man-made or a mixture of the two?), washing instructions, when to press and when not to press or block. So keep at least one of these bands and place in a small notebook along with a sample of the wool. That way you'll know exactly how to wash your finished project without fear of it shrinking or growing! If the item is a gift for someone, enclose a band with it so they will know how to care for that project you have slaved over.

Protect those points

Many of us, when in the middle of a project, simply push our needles through the ball of wool when finished for the day. Yes, this keeps your needles together, however each time you push those needles into the ball, the wool is damaged. It is far better to invest in a pair of point protectors or if you drink the odd bottle of wine then use a soft cork instead. For ease pierce two holes with a bradawl and away you go.

Charity begins at home

Patterns can be a bit pricey, so next time you walk past a thrift/charity shop pop in and have a look at what they have. You'll be surprised what they have hidden away. Do this on a regular basis and always look at the same section, chat to the volunteers who work in the shop and they'll soon start to put things by for you.

66 The biggest joy there is, is to make a piece of string into something you can wear. **99**

A little extra

When you make a garment with wool and you put a band from that wool into your 'washing' book why not also add extra information? For example what were the results of your tension swatch, how did the wool handle and what problems if any did you find? Then next time you use the same wool you'll know what you're letting yourself in for.

The lighter side of life

Always work in good light. This will obviously help your eyes and reduce eye strain but it should also help your overall finish, as you will hopefully make fewer mistakes. If you have to work at night or on a day that is dull and overcast then invest in a daylight simulation bulb.

Safe storage

Work with a tea-towel or similar on your lap and you can wipe your fingers and the needles at the end of each row, to keep both clean as you work. When you've finished for the day place your work into a large sealable bag and out of direct sunlight, to ensure it doesn't fade.

Two's a crowd

If you are working with two strands of wool then pass them both through a wide drinking straw. This should stop them becoming tangled as you work.

Waste not want not

If you plan ahead and purchase enough wool then you should find you'll have a little wool left over. Don't throw away these oddments; keep them and when you have a chance, turn them into an item that can help a local charity. Baby clothes for premature babies, doggy coats for an animal charity, dolls or toys for a children's charity, jumpers for ex-battery chickens (http://littlehenrescue.co.uk/jumpers.aspx) or sell the items at a local market to raise funds. If you're looking for inspiration then check these sites:

For knitting:

- http://www.lionbrand.com

- http://www.freepatterns.com

- http://www.dailyknitter.com

- http://www.warmwoolies.org/patterns.html

For crochet:

- http://www.crochetpatterncentral.com

- http://www.allfreecrafts.com/crochet/index.shtml

- http://www.craftown.com/crochet.htm

- http://www.freevintagecrochet.com

CRAFTY FACT

Originally crochet was not worked as one continuous piece. Instead you would work to the end of the row, break off the thread then start again at the beginning of the previous row. It was considered crude crocheting if you could see the back of the stitches.

Have a go with bamboo

If you're knitting all the time and you find your hands become easily tired, why not try a pair of bamboo needles? They are usually sold in sets, in a handy roll-up folder. They tend to be gentler on the hands, although they do take a little getting used to. They are generally longer than metal needles so are handy for larger projects.

Loop the loop

When you stop crocheting simply make the last loop larger and stick your ball of wool through it, that way your project should not start to unravel. Or you could use a nappy/diaper pin. Place the large pin inside the stitch (the one currently on the hook) and close it.

I must do my exercises

When working, stop those cramps by breaking for a moment and place your palms together with your elbows out. Then try to bring the elbows up slightly. This will stretch the tendons in the underarm, and relieve those aches and pains.

No repeats here

Whenever you go shopping take an index card that contains all the sizes of hooks and colors and types of wool you have stashed at home. That way you'll not end up with two hooks the same size.

What color?

Would you really like to mix and match your colors but are afraid you'll make a mistake? Take a trip to the local DIY store and invest in a color wheel. This will help you work out which colors go with each other and which ones don't. They're also very portable so you can take them along with you when you go on a shopping trip.

Will it stretch?

Before you purchase any wool type or make you are unfamiliar with, check its recovery. Take around 6" (15cm) and stretch it between your hands. If it does not return to the original size then you know it is unlikely to hold its shape, which means your garment will soon become misshapen.

A little on the side

The selvage of your knitted project is as important as the rest of your work. If you know you'll be joining your pieces together edge-to-edge then a single chain edge is ideal. However if you intend on backstitching your pieces together then a single garter edge may be more appropriate. If you're not joining edges (for example when making a scarf) then choose double garter edge.

Is it enough?

Nearing the end of your wool? Finish the row you are working on and then mark the halfway point of the wool left using a paperclip, then work your next row. If, when you've completed the next row, you still have at least 10" (25cm) left before you reach the paperclip then you know you have enough wool left for another row.

Don't get lost

When following a complicated pattern (for example Aran) with a lot of rows that are repeated try using a spiral notepad. Write out each row in large letters, one row per page. As you complete each row, turn the page and secure with an elastic band. This will make it easier to follow the instructions and you'll always know which row you are on, even if you have to walk away from your project for a while.

Don't struggle

If you find a pattern hard to read, blow it up to A3 size on a photocopier. This will make it easier to follow and you can also mark with a highlighter as you work.

Said no to novelty?

If you have always steered clear of funky wools (for example eye-lash yarn) because you find it difficult to see the stitch then why not try crocheting or knitting with two wools at a time? Match the funky wool with a thin wool and choose a slightly larger needle. In this way you should be able to see the stitch far easier as well as any mistakes you make.

Knitting needle sizes

Knitting needles and crochet hooks come in a range of sizes, so if you're unsure if that metric size 2.25mm will do the job then the tables on the following pages should help.

Please note that the tables are based on the best information available. Some charts on websites and books do vary slightly, so if possible stick to the metric size for hooks as that can't change.

Knitting needle sizes

Metric size (mm)	US size	UK and Canadian size
2.0	0	14
2.25	1	13
2.75	2	12
3.0		11
3.25	3	10
3.5	4	
3.75	5	9
4.0	6	8
4.5	7	7
5.0	8	6
5.5	9	5
6.0	10	4
6.5	10½	3
7.0		2
7.5		1
8.0	11	0
9.0	13	00
10.0	15	000
12.0	17	
16.0	19	
19.0	35	
25.0	50	

Crochet hook sizes

Metric size (mm)	US size	UK and Canadian size
1.0		
1.5		
1.75		
2		14
2.25	B/1	13
2.5	-	12
2.75	C/2	-
3.0	-	11
3.25	D/3	10
3.5	E/4	9
3.75	F/5	-
4.0	G/6	8
4.5	-	7
5.0	H/8	6
5.5	I/9	5
6.0	J/10	4
6.5	K/10.5	3
7.0	-	2
7.5	-	-
8.0	L/11	0
9.0	M/13	00
10.0	N/15	000

Why not branch out and add a little extra interest to your woollen projects by learning a new skill? Over the next few pages we have included a range of techniques that are easy to learn, require simple tools and are a great addition to your crafting skills base.

Knitting Nancy

Many of us may remember this as a craft our mothers or grandmothers tried to teach us. It has a variety of names including French Knitting, Spool Knitting, Corking and Knitting Knobby. It is a great wool craft to re-learn and allows you to create ties and much, much more using a small Knitting Nancy and a crochet hook.

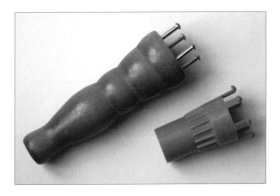

How to use a Knitting Nancy

1. Thread the end of the yarn through the Knitting Nancy from top to bottom.

2. Cast on by winding the yarn around one nail at a time, working around the top of the Nancy.

3. Now wrap the yarn around all of the nails (around the outside).

4. Using a fine crochet hook lift each loop up and over the nail, so that the loop becomes 'caught' by the thread you have just wrapped.

5. Continue to work in this way and eventually the knitting will appear at the bottom of the Knitting Nancy.

6. Once the knitting is long enough, cut the yarn to approximately 4″ (10cm) and thread through each loop, then pull tightly to complete.

The samples shown in our photograph show four pegs, however spools can be purchased with a far greater number of pegs. Mechanical Nancies can also be purchased where you simply crank the handle and the knitting is done for you. YouTube has a good number of videos showing this technique, one of which shows how a toilet roll and popsicle sticks can be used to create your own simple loom.

Flower looms

These little looms are easy to use and allow you to create fun flowers that can be used to make a complete project or add a little decoration.

How to use a flower loom

1. Tie a small loop in the yarn and place onto an outside peg.

2. Take the yarn over to the opposite peg and wrap around the peg.

3. Now bring the yarn back to the first peg and wrap around this peg, forming a figure of eight.

4. Take the yarn to the peg next to the second peg and wrap around this.

5. Bring the yarn back across the loom to the peg directly opposite the peg you have just wrapped around.

6. Continue in this way working around the loom until all pegs hold three loops.

7. Push the loops down, so they sit tightly on top of one another.

8. Wrap the end of the yarn around a peg once or twice to temporarily secure or place into the small slot at the base of the loom (many looms have this).

9. Cut a length of yarn and thread through a needle then secure by using a back stitch, working between each peg to create 'petals'.

10. Knot off securely then gently push the flower from the back to ease it off the loom.

11. Cut any ends to neaten.

Pot holder weaving

This type of weaving allows you to create woven squares which can be used as a centerpiece for a project or sewn together to create a completed project.

How to pot holder weave

1. Tie a knot around 2" (5cm) from the end of the yarn and place in the anchor slit in the base.

2. Take the yarn to the first peg opposite and wrap around the back. Bring the yarn back to the opposite peg.

3. Continue in this way until you have worked the length of the loom.

4. Take the loom threader and weave, with the hook end first under two threads, over two threads starting in the corner with the anchor slit.

5. Catch the yarn into the hook and gently pull the hook back through the yarns.

6. When the yarn has been 'woven' through all the strands catch it onto a peg.

7. Continue in this way until you have woven across the width of the loom.

8. To cast off pick up the first loop on the first peg using a crochet hook.

9. Pick up the loop on the second peg and slip the first loop over the second.

10. Continue in this way working around the loom.

11. When you reach the last loop take the yarn in the anchor slip and pass through the last loop to complete, pulling on the yarn.

This form of weaving works well when you use different types of yarns for the warp and the weft. This technique is ideal if you wish to use up all those half balls of yarn you have stashed away.

Finger knitting

This is a great technique to learn and is ideal for when you are on the go and cannot take your needles with you, because as the name suggests you simply need your fingers and a ball of yarn.

How to finger knit

1. Tie a slip knot at the end of the yarn and place over your little finger.

2. Now wind the yarn under and over your other fingers.

3. Wrap the yarn around the index finger and wind the yarn under and over your fingers ensuring the yarn is over a finger it went under the previous time.

4. Take the yarn across the front of the hand so it is nearer the tips of the fingers than the yarn wrapped around your fingers.

5. Carefully slip, one at a time, the loops on the fingers over the yarn placed over the hand.

6. Repeat this process and occasionally gently pull on the knitting.

7. Continue until you have created the length of knitting required.

8. To cast off, cut the yarn approximately 4" (10cm).

9. Take the loop furthest from the end of the yarn over to the next finger then slip the bottom loop over this.

10. Repeat this working across the hand and on the last loop pull the end of the yarn through and pull tight.

This technique works well with eyelash yarn or similar and the finished result can be used as a trim for both clothes and household accessories.

Hairpin lace

This is an age-old craft and can be used to create a wide range of projects from using as a trim to making complete garments. It is perhaps the hardest of the techniques covered here but it is well worth learning and is sure to give hours of fun.

How to use a hairpin lace loom

1. If the loom you are using has cross bars then remove one of the cross bars.

2. Create a loop at the end of your yarn, so the knot sits in the middle of the loom.

3. Pass the yarn around the right side of the loom and across the back, wrapping the yarn around the edge of the loom.

4. Insert your crochet hook into the loop and pick up the yarn and pull through the loop, this is your first chain.

5. Remove the hook from the loop and take it to the back of the loom and put the hook back through the loop.

6. Turn the loom over (turning right over left) and as you do wrap the yarn around the loom.

7. Insert your crochet hook into the loop and pick up the yarn and pull through the loop.

8. Continue in this way until you have created the length of hairpin lace you require.

If the strip you wish to create is longer than the loom you are working on and the loops become too tightly packed, then remove the bottom bar and slip off some of the hairpin lace.

This is perhaps not the easiest of the techniques we have included here but videos showing this as a step-by-step process can be viewed on YouTube. Also, as with many traditional forms of craft, there are a number of ways to work and some of the videos demonstrate a slightly different method of working to the one covered in this book.

Pom-poms

Pom-poms are a great addition to a range of projects and can be created using all those small oddments of yarn. Pom-pom makers can either be purchased or you can create your own using a couple of greeting cards. Simply create two circles of card with smaller circles cut out in the middle and away you go.

How to make a pom-pom

1. Place both sections of the pom-pom maker together (or your two pieces of card if you have created your own).

2. Wind off a small amount of yarn.

3. Hold the end of the yarn and begin to wind around the pom-pom maker going through the hole.

4. Keep winding around and through the hole until it is impossible to pass further yarn through the hole.

5. Using a sharp pair of scissors cut around the outer edge.

6. Carefully pull the pom-pom maker apart, just enough to wrap a piece of yarn around the middle, which is tied off securely.

7. Carefully pull the pom-pom maker off. If you have created your own you can carefully cut off.

8. Roll the pom-pom in your hand then trim any strands that are slightly too long to neaten up.

If you wish to speed things up slightly then wind a double yarn around the pom-pom maker. This also allows you to mix two different textures or colors and wind them on at the same time.

Stick weaving

Who would believe that by using just five small sticks you could actually weave a strip of 'fabric'? They are simple to use and come in a variety of forms. The strips made from them can be sewn together to create wider strips or you could use them as part of a knitted or crocheted item.

How to stick weave

1. Cut as many strands of yarn as you have sticks, three times the length of strip you are going to make.

2. Thread each strand of yarn through the hole of each weaving stick so the stick is in the middle of the strand. These will become your warp threads.

3. Place the sticks next to one another.

4. Tie off the ends making sure that each end is tied to an end that originates from an adjacent stick.

5. Take the end of the ball of yarn and tie the end to one of the outside sticks, this will become your weft thread.

6. Begin to weave the yarn in and out of (up and over) the sticks bringing the yarn around the last stick.

7. Continue to weave and as the sticks fill up carefully push the woven yarn down the sticks and onto the warp threads.

8. Keep weaving in this way until you have woven the length of strip required.

9. Adjust the weaving to ensure it is evenly spaced.

10. Finally cut the warp threads near the holes in the sticks and tie off all the threads to complete.

Cross Stitch & Embroidery

❝ Housework comes after cross stitch and embroidery. Don't believe me? Then take a quick look in the dictionary. **❞**

Chapter 4
Cross Stitch & Embroidery

Cross stitch and embroidery are very popular crafts with many, many magazines, books and websites devoted to them. The great thing about these crafts is they are very portable, costs can be kept very low (in comparison with other crafts) and devotees can keep projects as simple or as complicated as they want. The following tips hopefully include something for everyone, from the novice to the crafter who has practiced for a while and is ready to learn a few new tricks.

In the beginning

If you have never cross stitched before then pick a design on 14 count Aida fabric. Make sure your chosen design uses whole cross stitches, as these are the easiest ones to start with. Also try to pick a small design as it's more satisfying to finish a design in a few days than one that takes weeks or even months.

Add a little extra

Why not add a little extra dimension to your work by adding ribbon, beads or even rhinestones? They not only add texture but also depth to your design and are easy to work with.

Park it!

If you are working on a small project that is made up of several different colors save yourself some time and thread up a needle in each color. Then simply 'park' each needle on one side of your project out of the way, so it is waiting for you when you need it.

Tension trouble

Depending on our mood our stitching tension will vary from day to day. When working with small blocks of color this difference in tension will not be visible. However, if working on a large block of color this difference in tension will become visible. So try to allow yourself enough time to work the complete block so this change in tension is not visible.

Swap shop

Have you lost heart with a project which has been sitting around for months, perhaps even years? Then why don't you form a group of stitchers who perhaps meet once a month? You can then share time together swapping advice and these unloved projects. A project you have lost heart in may be just the project someone else is looking for. That way you'll be sure it gets the love and attention it deserves.

Small things

Have a small amount of fabric or thread left? Don't throw it away – make yourself some small samples. They make great gift tags or center pieces for greeting cards. Place them in small gilt frames which can then be hung on the wall or perhaps even a doll's house.

All together now

When working on a few small projects do not cut out each one separately, as this can be a waste of fabric. Work each one on a larger piece leaving a margin around each design then cut out once finished. This should cut down on the final amount of wasted material.

Rough around the edges

When working with any fabric the edges of the fabric will fray. In order to stop this, overstitch the edges by hand or if you're lucky enough to own one, use an overlocking machine. The small amount of time invested will cut down on the frustration of those long pieces of thread coming away from the edge and getting wrapped around your hands as you work. If you don't have a home sewing machine then you could try a product called Fray Stop®. Available in a small plastic bottle, you squeeze the Fray Stop® around the edges and as the name suggests it should stop that nasty fraying.

Getting the needle

We've all done it, run out of time and tucked the needle into the fabric for safe keeping. However if you leave the project for a while and it manages to get a little damp sometimes cheaper needles can rust, leaving a mark in your work. To avoid this, sew a small plastic bag to the corner of the work or a frame (if you are using one) which is sealable. You can then pop your needle into this without fear of marking your project.

Rid that rust

If you leave a needle in your work and it gets damp you can get a small rust mark. Now believe it or not cream of tartar can save the day. Simply dampen the stain and spread a little cream of tartar over the top. Allow it to sit for a while then rinse off with tepid water. If the stain is small, cover the stain with the cream of tartar then hold over the steam from a boiling kettle (keeping fingers well out of the way). As soon as the stain is removed rinse the project straight away.

Bigger is best

Try to use a hoop that is larger than the finished design and before you start ensure you mark up the middle of the fabric, so you start in the middle. That way you'll not have to move the project around the frame whilst working. This will cut down on the chance of pulling the fabric out of shape and also squashing the stitches in the frame.

Can I have a go Mom?

Try not to leave your new project lying around where the children can get hold of it. This simply puts temptation in their way. Invest in a cheap kit for children and let them sit beside you as you stitch. Or gather together some of your oddments and let them have a go on these. They'll enjoy creating their own masterpiece and it will cut down on the possibility of them 'spoiling' your current project.

Don't get cross get even!

When working in cross stitch ensure you work all the stitches in the same direction. So if your first bar of the stitch is bottom left to top right, all your first stitches should be in this direction. In this way your finished piece will look wonderfully even. One way to ensure this is to complete a row of 'first stitches' in the color you are working then return in the opposite direction to complete the stitch.

" I cannot count my day complete 'til needle, thread and fabric meet. "

Prior to 1804 needlework patterns were simple outlines without a grid. However in this year a print seller in Berlin by the name of Phillipson introduced blocked and colored patterns on a square grid, with each square representing a stitch. The patterns were made from copperplate prints then hand painted. Until that time this technique had only been used by weavers and had never been adapted for needlepoint.

Upside-down

Sometimes charts can be difficult to follow. One method to make reading the chart easier is to turn both the chart and the project upside-down. Charts tend to use symbols and when working from one you are often following a 'shape' rather than each individual symbol. By turning the graph and project upside-down the 'shape' being followed becomes clearer, making it easier to read.

Bead-dazzled

When adding beads to your design always use a thread that is similar in color to the beads you are using. When working onto a cross stitch design (using a double thread) bring the needle up through the fabric, thread through the bead onto the thread and then pass back down. This will be the first half of your cross stitch. Then bring the needle back up and work the second half of the cross stitch allowing one strand of thread to go either side of the bead.

CRAFTY FACT

In 1964 the fossilized remains of a Cro-Magnon hunter (30,000 BC) were found in Sungir near Vladimir, Russia. His fur clothing, boots and hat were heavily decorated with hand stitched horizontal rows of ivory beads. This is perhaps the oldest sample of bead embroidery.

Keep it neat at the back

When you begin any new project you will need to bring the thread up from the back of the fabric. If you use a knot to anchor your thread in place you'll be adding bulk. Therefore why not try one of these methods instead?

Waste knot

Knot the end of your thread. Take it down though your fabric around 1" (2.5cm) from your starting point. Work your stitches and as you do, catch in the thread held in place by the knot. Then when secure simply cut the thread back.

Hold and weave

Hold around 1" (2.5 cm) of thread at the back of the fabric whilst you make your first few stitches. As you bring the needle back through to the back catch this loose end into the back of the stitching which secures it in place without adding bulk.

Loop knot

If you're using two strands of thread, start with one strand twice as long as you need. Fold it in half and thread the needle so the two ends of the thread are near the needle and the 'loop' is the end farthest from the needle. Pull the needle up through the fabric but do not pull the thread completely through. Then when you take the needle back down pass it through the loop. This will successfully anchor your thread in place without the use of a knot.

In the end

As with beginning a new stitch, when finishing do not knot off the thread to anchor in place. Ensure you have a reasonable amount of thread still in your needle then run the end of the thread through the back of the same color stitches. Once the thread has travelled through the back of around four to six stitches, remove the needle then snip the thread close to the last stitch.

Roll with it

When you've finished a project that is not on a frame don't fold it to store, as this can introduce folds or kinks into the fabric. Simply place a clean white cloth and roll your project instead (an old clean bed sheet cut down to size is often useful). If you are working on a smaller project place it inside an old pillow case and roll that. Then tuck it away in a workbox or a drawer. That way it'll keep stain and dust-free.

Sensational stencils

If you are working a simple design and want to add a little extra interest then create an interesting background by stenciling or painting a simple design on your fabric before you start. Stencils can be purchased from many good craft shops in a range of themes and dry stencil paints are easy to apply using stiff- bristled brushes. If you are a little more confident try painting in a background.

Rebellious ribbon

Working with ribbon can produce the most amazing results in a very short time. However if you find the ribbon a little rebellious it can be easily untwisted by lifting and manipulating it with the needle. Do try to keep your ribbon flat during working to avoid any unnecessary kinks. When pulling the ribbon through the fabric try to pull gently to allow the ribbon to lie softly on top of the fabric, do not pull on it too much otherwise you'll find the shape you are trying to create will be lost.

Leave it out

If you have a diagram or chart for a large design remember you don't have to do the whole thing. Take a small element from the design and use it to create your own project. No one will ever know. Well, as long as you don't tell them!

Which way round?

Did you know that the method of creating a needle actually gives it a wrong and right side? So if you are unable to thread the needle try turning it around.

CRAFTY FACT

1830 to 1840 was the heyday for the printed colored chart with new designs being published all the time. In 1840 alone it is estimated that 14,000 new designs were released and that particular firm had 1,200 women hand coloring patterns.

Out damn spot, out!

It's inevitable you are going to prick your finger and, if you're really unlucky, manage to get blood onto your project. Rather than allowing the blood to dry it should be removed immediately. Take a small length of sewing thread, roll it into a ball and dampen it in your mouth. Take a piece of folded tissue paper or kitchen towel and place it on the back of the fabric. Then blot the offending blood stain on the front with the ball of thread. The enzymes in your saliva will react with your blood and dissolve it. Remember to dab, do not rub, and be patient; it may take two or three attempts to remove completely.

By the light of day

Many of us don't have the luxury of sewing during the day, so we find ourselves sewing when the sun has gone down. In order to reduce the possibility of eye strain and reduce the chances of you picking the wrong shade/color, invest in a good quality daylight bulb.

CRAFTY FACT

It is believed the word 'embroidery' comes from the Anglo-Saxon word for edge although the technique is much older than that. Originally the word was first applied to decoratively stitched borders on medieval church vestments but down the centuries it covered all stitched decoration on any textile fabric.

Subscribe

There is a myriad of good magazines available and many of them offer a subscription service. These are a good investment for a number of reasons:

- You'll never miss an issue

- Subscription normally means you get the magazine for slightly less and you'll not be paying postage

- Many offer great deals, and freebies are offered to those who subscribe

Old Mother Hubbard

When you buy your stock always ensure you buy more than enough. Like many things in life thread comes in dye lots and there is nothing worse than getting almost to the end of a project to find you have run out and so has the shop!

White's alright

If you are in a hurry and are working on a project that has a lot of white in it, rather than working the white in stitches simply leave these out. Once framed no one will notice and you'll not only save yourself time but also thread!

" Embroidery is the art of enriching fabric with stitchery. **"**

Jump a little bit higher now

Sometimes you'll get stitches that are all on their own; these are called 'loners.' Now the rules state that you shouldn't run your thread or jump (as it's called) more than four stitches. So what do you do?

- If the loner is amongst others of a different color you could use the loop stitch then anchor off by running the stitch under the others around it. This only works well if the color surrounding the loner stitch is darker.

- You could work the stitch using just one strand (most patterns state you use two strands). Work the first half of the stitch twice then the second half of the stitch twice. Once this has been done simply knot the two single ends. Although you are breaking the no knot rule, it'll be half the size because you only used one strand.

- If the loner is not surrounded by other stitches you could place a piece of lightweight fabric behind the project whilst you are working. Then when you carry your thread across it will not show through the front of your project.

- You could adapt the pattern by leaving out the loner stitch or adding a few more around it. Only those who see the pattern will know what you've done.

- Lastly remember that just as in life rules are meant to be broken. So if the thread is light in color and the stitch is not too far away from the group you are working on then go on, be a devil and break the no jumping rule.

CRAFTY FACT

The earliest known dated sampler was stitched by an English girl called Jane Bostocke, in 1598. The sampler contains floral and animal motifs, patterns, different types of stitches and an alphabet (which does not include the letters J, U and Z).

Finishing touch

It does not matter how careful you are, by the time you've finished a project there will be a mark or two. They can be removed quite easily if the whole piece is placed in cool soapy water. Use a mild soap that is designed for delicates, or invest in a liquid cleaner sold in many good craft stores. Once you have cleaned the project lay it on a clean towel, on a rack if possible, and allow it to dry naturally. If you are going to do this then before washing undertake a color test with the threads you used. Simply put a couple of stitches in the middle of some waste fabric and wash it to see what happens.

Iron

Sometimes you may wish to iron your completed project to improve the finish. Place the work onto a clean dry towel, face down and place a piece of acid-free tissue paper over the work whilst you are ironing. In this way you'll not snag the stitching which could ruin an otherwise faultless piece.

Grid

When following a pattern why not grid your fabric for ease? Baste/tack using a bright colored thread every ten squares if you are using Aida or every twenty threads if you are using even-weave fabric. When using this method do ensure the thread you are using is smooth and will completely pull out of the fabric and not leave small tufts behind. If you are unsure carry out a little test baste/tack first.

It's a dirty job

When placing your project onto a frame attach with some acid free white tissue paper as well. Simply place the tissue paper over your fabric then place both onto your frame. When the fabric is in place, carefully cut a hole in the paper, where the design will be. In this way the tissue paper will protect the fabric during the sewing process.

It's a frame up

When you get an item framed ensure the framer uses only acid free board, so the work does not discolor over time, and that the work is pinned onto the board with rustproof pins or laced in place rather than with glue or staples. Hopefully in this way your hard work will last for generations to come and become an heirloom.

In the frame

If you are working with a frame and it only supports part of the work don't be tempted to leave the work in the frame between sewing sessions. It's likely the frame will distort the fabric and ruin your work.

CRAFTY FACT

Perhaps the oldest of all woven materials is linen and many cloth fragments dating as far back as 5,000 BC have been found in tombs in South America, Egypt and China, which show examples of darning, half cross stitch and satin stitch.

Get organized

When you're working on a project where you are following a chart with symbols try labeling the thread with the symbols for ease. Many kits provide you with a piece of card with holes along the edge. Place the thread in the holes and draw each symbol next to the corresponding thread. When working with lots of different shades that are similar try to do this during daylight hours. That way you'll not make a mistake and put the wrong shade with the wrong symbol.

Backstitch

When adding backstitch to your design add it after you have removed your work from the canvas. However if you prefer to add backstitch whilst the canvas is still in place, use Holbein stitch (double running stitch), to create a much neater line.

In the middle

Whether you grid your fabric or simply tack a cross on your fabric, always start in the center and work outwards. This will guarantee your finished design is centered.

Make it big

When working on a new design take a photocopy of the chart and if possible enlarge it. Then it'll be easier to see the symbols. You'll also be able to mark on the photocopy as you work where you've got to and avoid ruining your original chart.

How much border?

Refer to the key on the pattern you are working from to see what size the finished design will be on the fabric count you have chosen. Then cut your fabric at least 4″ (10cm) larger in all directions. For large designs allow at least 8″ (20cm) of border.

A knotty problem

To reduce the possibility of knots as you work cut your thread length to no longer than about 18″ (45cm). If you still get the occasional knot then use the tip of your needle to loosen the knot slightly and then pull the thread firmly. If this doesn't work then cut the thread below the knot, fasten off and start again.

" Oh, sew many projects, sew little time! **"**

Getting in a twist

As you work if you find your thread appears to be unraveling, stop stitching every so often and allow the needle to hang down and untwist before carrying on.

How much fabric do I need?

If you don't have a chart that tells you how much fabric you require, then simply count the number of stitches in each direction. Divide the number of stitches by the 'count' of the fabric and then add the correct amount for a border.

CRAFTY FACT

One of the oldest examples of a complete cross stitch design (although the crosses are upright) was discovered in a Coptic tomb in Upper Egypt dating from around 500 AD Thankfully the dry desert climate had preserved it.

What sizes are best?

When working on different Aida count fabric it is best to adjust not only the needle size you are working with but also the number of strands. The table below suggests suitable combinations:

Aida count	Needle size	How many strands
8	22	3 to 4
11	22	3
14	24	2 to 3
16	26	2
18	28	1
22	28	1

Frame

If you are new to cross stitch or embroidery it's very difficult to know what frame is right for you. So here is a list of the most popular:

Ring frames

These are ideal for smaller projects. The more expensive ring frames are 1″ (2.5cm) deep and may be wrapped in calico or muslin to prevent your project from slipping. When choosing a ring frame ensure the design fits inside the frame and allows for a good border around the design.

Scroll frames

These are great if you have a floor or table stand. The two scroll bars have a tape stapled along the edge of the bars, so you can pin or sew the fabric in place. The two side bars slot into the holes on each end of the scroll bars and are screwed on so the fabric is tight. The one disadvantage is that sometimes the screws become loose and so does the fabric. Also sometimes the side bars are short so some of the project may need to be rolled around the bars. This can leave creases on your project.

Slate frames

These are great for all-over tension. The main bars have tape stapled along the edge so you can pin/tack the fabric in place. The side arms slot into the holes on each end of the main bars and have holes drilled into them. These arms are pegged against the main bars so the fabric is very tight. The advantage of the slate frame is that once the arms have been pegged out the fabric will not become slack. The side arms tend to be slightly longer than scroll frames, so you may not have to roll your project as you work. These frames are ideal if you're going to be on a project for a long period of time.

Stretcher bar frames

The bars are sold in pairs, with the end of the bars having teeth so you can slot the bars together to form a square or rectangle frame. As you attach make sure you pull the fabric very tight. When mounting make sure you use lots of thumbtacks or staples; the closer they are the more tension you'll be able to get on the fabric, 1" (2.5cm) intervals are ideal.

Q-snap frames

These are fairly inexpensive and often made from plastic. The bars slot together and the fabric is clipped into the plastic frame by slotting another piece of plastic over the fabric. Unfortunately the fabric can slip in this type of frame and does not stay consistently tight. To reduce the fabric slipping wrap the bottom section using muslin/calico strips.

Candle Making

" Better to light a candle than to curse the darkness. "

Chapter 5
Candle Making

Since the dawn of time candles have been used to light the nights. Today although we can turn on a light with a flick of the switch, many people still return to the humble candle. They are used to create mood lighting or are used in many different religions to celebrate a variety of occasions. Today candles can be purchased in a dedicated candle store or found on the shelf in a local supermarket. However what could be more satisfying than making your own? To help you improve your candles here is a selection of fabulous candle making tips.

Pick your wax

Paraffin wax comes with different melting points, each suitable for a different type of project. So try to pick one that is right for what you want to make. For example a wax with a melting point of 127°F/52°C is great for container candles as it has a low melting point and holds scent until the candle is lit. A wax with a melting point of around 140°F/60°C is ideal for general candle making processes. A wax with a melting point of 145°F/63°C is great for carving and shaping, whilst a wax with a very high melting point of 176°F/80°C can be used for overdipping a candle, which will protect surface decoration such as stickers or photographs.

Caboom!

Wax should never be heated over a direct flame; you should use the double boiler method (one pan inside another which holds simmering water). When working with wax remember to keep an eye on the temperature, using a thermometer, as wax heated above 210°F/100°C can spontaneously ignite. If your wax does catch fire, switch the heat off at source and DO NOT move the pan. Smother with a damp cloth and allow it to fully cool before you move it.

It's the size that counts

When making candles you have to think about the width of the wick you will be using compared with the width of the candle. Although the burning of the wick is dependent on many different factors (wax chosen, percentage of additive used etc.) it is advisable to pick a width of wick that is designed for the size of mold you are using. Most wicks are sold in lengths and these will be marked with a number in millimeters. This number refers to the width of the candle you intend on making, so use this as your guide.

CRAFTY FACT

Candles have been used by countless ancient civilizations to help them worship many gods. For example the Ancient Romans honored the God Saturn (god of fertility and agriculture) and the Druids honored their Sun God, Balder (the god of light, joy, Spring and peace).

Wicked wick

The wicking of rubber molds can be tricky, but with the aid of a wicking needle it becomes much easier. When 'wicking up' take care to ensure the needle goes through the very top of the mold. To avoid stabbing yourself, use a cork on the outside of the mold as you push the needle through rather than your fingers.

Quick wick

If you intend making quite a few candles from the same mold, then do not cut the wick to size. Simply wick up the mold using the entire ball of wick, leaving the excess wick at the head of the candle. Then, when the candle is cool, remove from the mold. As you pull the candle the wick will automatically follow, wicking up your mold ready for use the next time, all in one simple action.

Read all about it

As already mentioned wax will spill and you'll be surprised just how far it can travel. To help you clean up, cover your work surface with something that can be thrown away. Avoid using newspaper as this can leave print behind; use kitchen foil or baking parchment, both of which can be used a couple of times before having to be consigned to the bin. If using baking parchment ensure you keep it well away from naked flames.

Keep it safe

When making candles you're not only dealing with heat and hot water/wax you are also dealing with a material that is not good for the insides. Therefore keep children and pets out of the way and place candle making ingredients out of reach when not in use.

A drain on resources

It's a dilemma to know what to do with that wax in the bottom of your pot when you've finished your making session. Unless you really like calling in the plumber, don't pour wax down the sink/drain as it will block it. Simply pour the unused wax into a pot and save for another session.

Water bath

Sometimes you'll want to speed the cooling of your candle. Now there are two ways to do this. You can fill a flat bottomed container with cold water and stand your candle in it whilst still in the mold (but don't let any water get into the mold). Another method for cooling your candle quickly is to place it in the fridge. However care must be taken, as the shock of the different temperatures can cause the candle to crack.

"Any day candle making is a good day."

Please release me

Mold release is handy when releasing candles from rubber molds. If you don't have any you can make your own using dishwashing liquid and water, mixed 50:50. If you don't have dishwashing liquid then rub your rubber mold with a little talcum powder or cooking oil.

Boiled, fried or poached?

If you want to melt a little wax or a small amount of wax dye then have a rummage in your kitchen cupboards and find yourself an egg poacher. Just remember once used for candle making it is not suitable for cooking your eggs afterwards. Therefore be prepared to lose it to your candle making kit.

With a little support

Many molds come with their own wick supports. However if you don't get one then you can make one from items such as toothpicks, popsicle sticks or even pencils. Whilst the candle is setting you may find the wick support moves. To avoid this happening use a little mold seal at either end to anchor it in place.

Dear Diary

Keep a candle making diary and record your successes and failures. For example if you record how much wax a mold needs you won't have to keep working it out. Also keep a record of what wick you used, then when you burn the candle make a note of any problems that occur. All this information will help you improve your candle making skills.

It just won't budge

Sometimes you just can't get that candle to come out of the mold, so it needs a little help. Or try putting it in the fridge for 15-20 minutes or stand it in hot water for 10 minutes or so. That should get it moving!

Cute bottom

If you find you have an untidy bottom (on your candle!) then use a small travel iron (without holes in the base plate) to neaten it. Or place a flat baking tray on a very low heat on the stovetop and smooth the bottom of the candle over it. The heat will melt the base and neaten it all at once.

Shocking stocking

If the outside of your candle or the base needs a little shine then take an old stocking, place it over the tip of your finger and rub. For an improved finish try working in one direction up and down the sides of the candle or in a smooth circular motion around the base.

Make your own

To save money you don't have to use shop purchased molds, you can make your own. As long as the item is watertight and can take hot wax then it'll do. When using ceramics or glass objects remember to warm them first in the oven so the heat of the wax does not cause them to crack. Also remember the opening of the object has to be larger than the base, otherwise you'll not get the candle out!

CRAFTY FACT

More candles are sold during the third quarter of the year because of their link to religious festivals including Christmas, Hanukkah and Kwanzaa.

Sweet smell of success

Scent can be added to the candle during the making process and there are special perfumes just for this purpose. These perfumes are very strong, so only a few drops are required. However if you don't add this perfume during the making process it's not too late to have a scented candle.

You could try adding an essential oil to the well of wax as the candle burns. You'll also get the properties of the essential oil as the candle burns, for example Bergamot is a great pick-me-up, Citronella keeps insects at bay, Eucalyptus is ideal for unblocking noses, Lavender is calming and aids rest and Rosemary helps concentration. NOTE: Care should be taken when choosing an essential oil as some can be harmful to pregnant women.

Chunky

To add extra interest to a candle, add chunks of wax to the mold before pouring in the clear wax. Pre-cut chunks are available that are specially formulated for this type of candle. However if you want to make your own chunks, this is easily done. Place some kitchen foil into a baking tray; melt some wax, stearin and color as desired. Pour this onto the sheet of kitchen foil and allow it to cool. Once cool, break the wax into chunks or cut using a knife. Try not to make the chunks too small, the ideal size is about ¾" (2cm). Dark colored chunks encased in light/clear wax tend to create more successful chunk candles.

Pour baby pour

Another way to add interest to a candle is to create one that has two or even three colors, one encased within the other. Basically you pour in the wax, allow a crust to form, pour it out, then add your second color (this is known as a pour in, pour out candle).

When making this form of candle it is advisable to use a darker color wax for the interior layer, keeping the outside clear or a light color. The longer you leave the first pouring to set then the thicker the outer layer will be, thus affecting how much and how strong the inner color appears. The ideal temperature for pouring your wax is between 175°F/80°C and 180°F/82°C.

Going for a dip

Candles can be created by dipping a wick into molten wax repeatedly. Dipping cans can be expensive, so if you want to experiment with this technique then use a large food can. They are a cheap alternative that can be used time and again.

Hot under the collar

It is important to keep an eye on the temperature of the wax not only for perfect candles but also for safety. Therefore you should always have a thermometer to hand. If you're unable to source a candle-making thermometer then use a jam-making one instead. They often have a scale showing the correct heat range for candle making.

Old for new

If you are recycling old candles, remove all burnt pieces and old wick. Remember if the candle was originally made in a plastic mold it will have stearin in it. It is therefore advisable to make your new candle using a plastic rigid mold rather than a rubber mold, so you don't ruin your rubber molds.

Sagging bottom

As the wax cools it will often dip around the wick, leaving an unsightly well in the base. To overcome this problem you should 'top up'. This is done when a crust around 1/8" (5mm) has formed. Pierce the crust using a cocktail stick or similar then top up the well using the same colored molten wax. If you don't prick the surface of the crust then it is possible for the 'top up' section to fall out later.

Stuck on you

There are a couple of reasons why a candle will not come out of a mold: firstly, your mold may have been dirty from the last casting. So always clean a mold before using with hot soapy water or a mold cleaner, which is available from many good candle-making equipment suppliers. Alternatively you may have over-filled your candle when you were topping up and allowed wax to seep down the outside edge of your candle. In order to stop this happening, care must be taken when topping up.

"A creative mess is better than tidy idleness."

Basic candle making kit

Thankfully candle making is one of the few crafts/hobbies which, when you take your first faltering steps, is inexpensive. You may already have many of the items in your home.

- Wax – perhaps wax pellets with a medium melting point are best for the novice candle maker to invest in. At a later date other melting points can be experimented with and other types of candles created

- Double boiler or two pans (one which will sit comfortably inside the other)

- Egg poacher, great for melting dye

- Wax dye in a variety of colors

- Scales

- Thermometer – if you are unable to purchase a candle-making thermometer then a jam one should serve you well

- Scissors sharp enough to cut wick

- Selection of different widths of wick - the label will tell you which width of wick to use with which width of candle

- Selection of shop purchased molds

- Selection of home-made molds for example the little plastic tubs microwavable puddings come in

- Old clothes to wear during the making process

- Wicking needle will help you wick up all manner of molds

- Wick supports to hold the end of the wick whilst you are pouring the wax into the mold

- Mold seal to seal around the wick at the base of your mold

- Wick sustainers used to anchor wicks in glass containers

- Pliers to attach a wick sustainer to your length of wick

Live a long life

After spending time making your candles you obviously want them to last as long as possible. There are a few ways to improve the burning life of a candle, which include keeping the wick trimmed to 1/8" (5mm), snuffing out rather than blowing out, burning out of a draught and cooling it in a fridge (well wrapped in a plastic bag) prior to lighting.

Decoration

There are a number of ways you can decorate your candles which include twisting decorative wire around them with beads, applying candle appliqué motifs (available from any good candle making supplier), using appliqué sheets (again available from any good candle making supplier), hitting the surface of the candle gently with the head of a hammer to make an indent, or creating designs using a burning tool used for the process of Pyrography (decorative wood burning).

Carpet burns

To remove spilled candle wax from your carpet (or other fabrics) cover the affected spot with a brown paper bag or a piece of brown paper and run across the top of it with a medium-hot iron.

CRAFTY FACT

It is believed the word candle comes from the word 'candela' derived from the word 'candeo' which means to burn and was probably introduced into the English language as early as the 8th century.

Floating candles

If you only have a small amount of wax and want to use it up then have a go at making floating candles. They can be easily made by lining patty or mini-muffin tins with foil. Pour in the wax, cut wick to length then poke into the candle once the crust has formed. Easy!

Roll with it

Another great way of creating candles is to use beeswax sheets. These are simply rolled around a dipped wick. Once mastered, this technique allows you to create candles in minutes! If you find during the rolling process the sheets begin to crack then warm with a hair drier for a couple of minutes or place in a warm environment, for example an airing cupboard or a warm oven (don't leave for too long!).

Water bath

If you are making a large number of candles and are using a water bath you may find after time the water starts to warm. Rather than pour all that precious water away add a few ice cubes to cool it back down.

CRAFTY FACT

It's believed the first candle was perhaps a lump of animal fat (tallow) with a wick made from plant matter stuck into it. Traces of such candles have been found around the world in caves inhabited by early man.

Striped success

When creating striped candles, timing is very important. If your layers are allowed to become too cold then it is possible that the stripes will come apart when you remove the candle from the mold. To help the stripes adhere to one another, use a wicking needle or cocktail stick to pierce the layer before you pour the next in.

Go green

Try making candles with soy wax. It's completely natural and biodegradable. It's non-toxic and is actually edible prior to color and scent being added. It burns at a lower heat than paraffin wax, so your finished candles last longer and give off less soot. Different manufacturers give different instructions for their wax, so read the instructions carefully.

Crimp your style

When creating candles using combustible inclusions, use a small crimp (normally used in jewelry making) and place it around the wick as a safety precaution. Place it just above the items, so the candle snuffs itself out before it reaches them.

Clean as you go

Sometimes at the end of a candle-making session there will be wax left on your mold. A craft heat gun is ideal for melting the wax. You can then remove most of the unwanted wax with a quick wipe of a tissue. Ensure you don't touch the mold with the tip of the heat gun as this could damage the mold.

How to store

Candles should be stored in a cool, dark, dry place and tapers should be stored flat to prevent warping.

Showing them off

When making a simple arrangement of candles place them in odd numbers of three, five or seven as these numbers seem to be more pleasing to the eye. When displaying floating candles, theme the color of the water to match your candles. Food dye is a cheap and safe way of coloring water. Also floating candles don't have to be the only items in the water. Many other objects can be added, for example flowers or colored ice cubes or perhaps colored glass beads or pretty stones. Finally, use distilled water to reduce the build-up of lime scale on the inside of the bowl.

Putting it out

Put out the flame on your candle by dipping the wick into the molten wax formed in the well. This should eliminate any smoking from the wick during the next burn, and always remember to re-center the wick. Also when burning a candle, try to allow a pool of wax to form across the top of the candle before extinguishing. This should make the candle burn longer and more evenly each time you light it.

What to add?

When using paraffin wax there are a number of additives that can help improve your finished candles. Here are the main ones:

Name of additive	Properties & How much to add
Stearin (palm oil/ stearic acid)	Aids the burning process and makes the wax shrink slightly to allow you to remove from the mold more easily. Stearin will attack the rubber in rubber molds
	Normally around 10% of weight of wax
Vybar	This comes in two forms which is dependent on the melting temperature of your wax. So you will need to match melting temperatures. This does not attack rubber, so use instead of stearin when using rubber molds
	Normally between 3% and 10% of weight of wax
Clear crystals	These allow you to create a more transparent candle. They are ideal when you wish to include items inside the main body of the candle
	Follow instructions on label, as amount needed varies with manufacturer

Name of additive	Properties & How much to add
Luster crystals	Make the colors of your candles come out brighter and also has the benefit that your candle will burn longer
	Follow instructions on label, as amount needed varies with manufacturer
UV inhibitor	This slows the fading process caused by sunlight but is unlikely to stop it. It is ideal for candles you know will be placed directly in the sun
	Follow instructions on label, as amount needed varies with manufacturer
Soft microcrystalline wax	This creates a sticky wax which is ideal when you wish to create candles with layers or similar
	Normally using 10% of total wax weight
Mineral oil	Allows you to create candles with a mottled look
	Follow instructions on label, as amount needed varies with manufacturer
Bees wax	This can be added to paraffin wax to improve the burn of the candle
	Normally 5% to 10% of total wax weight

Candle troubleshooting

Problem	Why	What to do
Candle is smoking	Your wick could be too large (thick)	Reduce the width of the wick used in your next batch
	You may have air pockets	Pour your wax at a hotter temperature
	Too much perfume has been added	Decrease the amount of scent used
	There is debris from a previous burn (i.e. match head)	Once a pool of wax has been formed remove debris
Candle is dripping	The wick is too small for the width of the candle	Choose a wider width of wick used in your next batch
	The wax is too soft	Cut down on the amount of additive used
Candle is burning too quickly	The wick is too small for the width of the candle	Choose a wider width of wick used in your next batch
	The wax is too soft	Cut down on the amount of additive used
Wick is drowning in well of wax around wick	The wick is too small for the width of the candle	Choose a wider wick in your next batch

Problem	Why	What to do
Candle is burning unevenly	It is possible the candle is in a draft	Move candle
Candle splutters when burning	It is possible somewhere during the making process water got into the wax	The water could have entered the wick during cooling in the water bath, so ensure the hole in the mold is sealed completely
		Do not pass anything that can drip over the top of the mold as you work
Flame flickers during burning	The wick chosen is too large for the size of the candle	Reduce the width of the wick used in your next batch
	The wax is too hard	Use less additive in your next batch
	The candle could be in a small draft	Move the candle to another position

Jewelry Making

" Wearing jewelry takes people's mind off your wrinkles. **"**

Chapter 6
Jewelry Making

Jewelry never goes out of fashion, just the type of items we adorn ourselves with. I can remember in my youth wearing earrings so large, that when the wind caught them they came round and hit me in the face! I swore I would never wear them again, but I'm sure I will when they come back into fashion.

Jewelry making is a highly addictive hobby. To be honest, which hobby isn't once you've caught the bug? The next few pages include a range of hints, tips and ideas that will not only allow you to create fantastic items of jewelry for less but will also show you how to complete your items to a high standard. So get reading, then get making, that's what it's all about!

Odds and ends

Rather than storing all those odd beads together in one pot get several little pots or jars, label with a color theme and just pop the correct colored bead into each pot. In this way when the pot is full you'll have the beads already sorted and ready for your next project.

Felt

When working with small beads they can drive you to distraction as they roll all over the place. Working on a piece of craft felt will stop the beads from rolling and you'll get your project made in double quick time.

Kinky

If you're working with nylon thread and it's full of kinks then don't despair. Fill a bowl with hand hot water then place the nylon thread in it. Leave to soak for around ten minutes or so and hey presto; all those kinks will be gone.

Nail clippers

When working with tiger-tail or similar threads don't use a pair of scissors to cut the thread, try using a pair of nail clippers. They give a clean edge to the cut and, when out and about with your jewelry making kit, can be taken on public transport.

Inspiration

Try to get into the habit of keeping a small notebook and pencil wherever you go. Then when inspiration strikes or you see a piece of jewelry you know you could use as inspiration, you can write down a few key words or doodle a little sketch. That way you'll not get home then have to rack your brains trying to remember that killer idea.

Recycle

Rather than buying new beads why not take a trip to your local thrift, charity shop, boot fair or junk shop? You'll find loads of dated necklaces, bracelets and earrings that can be taken apart and made into great new jewelry. You may find some of the beads need a bit of a clean. This is easily done before you take the item apart. Place in an old colander and then into some warm soapy water (cheap shampoo works well) then agitate. To get into those little nooks use an old toothbrush. NOTE: Don't put 'pearls' into water as the coating often lifts off.

Fantastic elastic

If you find the ends of the elastic get a little sticky then rub with a little baby powder. Also to ensure knots do not come undone, a dab of clear drying craft glue will hold them securely in place.

Make your own jump rings

You always seem to run out of jump rings just when you need them. So why not make your own with a little wire, a knitting needle, wire cutters and nylon pliers. Simply wrap the wire around your chosen knitting needle then slip off, cut to form the rings and harden off with the nylon pliers. Cheap, simple and effective.

CRAFTY FACT

Did you know it's not just Hollywood fiction, pirates really did wear earrings. They believed that if their ears were pierced with precious metals such as silver and gold it improved their eye-sight.

Round not oval

Rather than pulling jump rings apart to slip them onto your project, give them a little twist instead. This not only makes them easier to work with but also cuts down on the possibility of them going out of shape. In this way you'll end up with round jump rings rather than egg shaped ones.

Weave it wide

If you wish to make a large piece of bead weaving but your loom is not wide enough simply weave several pieces then sew them together, edge to edge, to create a larger finished project.

Basic jewelry making kit

The tools for making jewelry can be very basic and once purchased will last you a lifetime if looked after. So to make up a basic kit you'll need:

- Scissors – for cutting thread

- Selection of beads and you can never have enough of these!

- A variety of jewelry findings such as clasps, crimps, jump rings, end fasteners, ear wires, headpins/eyepins, etc.

- Round nose pliers – help you create loops with ease

- Bull nose pliers – good for all manner of jobs

- Flat nose pliers – also good for a range of jobs

- Snipe nose pliers – great for manipulating wire

- Side cutters – used to cut wire cleanly

- Crimping pliers – to enable you to neatly and securely fix crimps onto wire

- Nylon tipped mallet – for ensuring wire holds its shape once you have completed your design

- Stretch elastic – for creating bracelets, it comes in a variety of thicknesses and colors

- Nylon bead thread – comes in a variety of thicknesses and colors

- Bead board – allows you to work out your own designs with ease

- Beading needles – have a fine eye to allow you to bead onto thread

- Small pots to keep your beads safely stored

- Bead reamer – to allow you to enlarge the hole on glass, ceramic and stone beads

- Large storage box – for all the above items

" I bead to keep the economy going. It is my duty to support craft shops and internet sites. "

Can't see what's in the pot

If the pots you are keeping your beads safe in do not allow you to see what treasure is hidden inside, it's worth sacrificing a bead by sticking it to the lid with a little dab of glue. A quick and easy way to tell what's in the pot!

CRAFTY FACT

During the early 20th century it was considered uncivilized for ladies to have pierced ears. So the screw back was invented and around the 1930s the clip-on was invented.

A knotty problem

When trying to tie a knot in the right position it'll often refuse to do as it's told. So in order to get that knot to do what you want, grab a large sewing needle. Then form the knot, place the tip of the needle in the knot and use this to slide the knot to the right position. Once in position pull on the end of the thread, remove the tip of the needle and your knot will be just where you want it.

Give me a double please

When weaving on a loom if your project is going to need a little extra strength (for example when making a bracelet) use a double thread on the outer two warp threads. This means if you're making a project that is five beads across, you would normally have six warp threads, but now you would need to set up your loom with eight warp threads.

Hide the ends

If you need to tie off a thread when weaving on a loom, then securely knot on the outside warp thread, and pass the needle back through the line of beads you have just created. Bring the needle up in the middle of the line, loop the thread around the warp thread and cut off. In this way the weft thread just cast off should not come undone and the end will be hidden from sight.

Warp factor

Some designs in bead weaving include beads on the warp threads, which are brought down when needed during the making process. Before you start to weave ensure the beads are at the end of the loom you are working towards or you could find you are working from the wrong end!

Threading problem

Do you find when threading your beads onto the string that after the first half dozen or so your thread starts to fray? This can be remedied with a small dab of glue on the end of the thread.

The end

In order to ensure the end of the necklace or bracelet does not scratch the wearer, try to ensure the last few beads (and the first) have a large enough hole for the end of the thread to be passed through twice. In this way you can pass the end of the thread back through the bead, therefore improving your finish.

A gift

If you're giving your creations away as presents then give them in style and make a gift bag or box for them. Or you could use a pair of earrings as part of the decoration on a greetings card. Then you have a card and present all in one!

CRAFTY FACT

In some states of India the number and type of bangles or bracelets worn by a woman denotes her marital status. For example in Bengal married women wear iron kada (bangles), in Punjab a bride wears choodas (ivory bangles in red and white in multiples of four) and in Maharashtra green bangles are worn by women at very important occasions.

Don't throw it

If you have small ends of 0.8mm wire left over, don't throw them away. Using some nylon jaw pliers remove any kinks and then use it to make jump rings or if long enough, eye pins.

Knotty problem

When creating jewelry using thread or string, you may have to knot it. The ideal knot for this job is the reef knot. Simply tie right over left then left over right and pull.

Crafty clay

Polymer clay beads can be very expensive, however creating your own is child's play. A small bead-making device which is simple to use, cheap and available from most outlets lets you 'roll' your own. The added bonus is that you'll be sure no one else has just the beads you've created, allowing you to create truly individual but identical sized beads.

It may be old

Macramé is an old craft which is simple to learn and great for creating necklaces and bracelets. Today thread is often cheap, and available in a huge range of colors and finishes, allowing you to create some really wonderful and individual projects.

Hole in one

When buying beads it is inevitable some will have a hole that is not big enough or will have a small imperfection which will rub and damage the thread during wear. This is a simple problem to overcome if you're working with glass, ceramic or stone beads. Simply invest in a bead reamer or two. These tools are normally diamond tipped for durability and precision made, which allows you to file a hole to make it larger and remove any of those rough edges. So a bead you would normally consign to the bin can be saved.

Use when wet

When using your bead reamer always use plenty of water as you work. If the reamer should become dry then the diamond coating will begin to strip away and it'll be ruined in no time. Also by keeping the reamer wet you protect your beads, as the water will reduce the heat generated by the friction as you work.

Loop the loop

When making loops on your pliers it is sometimes difficult to make them all the same size. To remedy this take a little masking tape and wrap around the pliers' jaws, marking where you wish to wrap the wire around. In this way each time you make a loop you simply lay the wire against the masking tape and your loops will be the same size each and every time.

Roll with it

It doesn't matter how hard you try, small beads always seem to jump off your lap or work surface and spend time on the floor or down the side of the sofa cushions. Retrieving these beads can be very frustrating. However if you invest in a little roller, the type you use to remove lint or pet hair, the job becomes a breeze. Simply roll it over the area you have been working in and it'll pick up all those stray beads. You then simply wipe off the beads gently onto a tray.

How long is a piece of string?

Knowing how many beads it'll take to create a string can be difficult to work out. So to calculate how many you'll need simply string a predefined length using your chosen beads, say 2" (10cm). Then count how many beads it took. You can then multiply this number to work out how many beads you'll need. This is also a great way of working out how many beads it'll take when you are working on a loom. Simply work up a square, again a predefined size, and then count how many you used.

" Dust is mind over matter...... I don't mind so it doesn't matter. **"**

Clear as day

When creating stretchy bracelets with clear elastic how often have you put it down then spent the next ten minutes trying to spot where it is? A simple way around this is to cut your elastic a little longer than you need then paint the ends with a bright nail varnish

What size?

When making bracelets it can be difficult to work out the sizes required. Solve this problem by using a piece of masking tape. Mark both ends of the correct length and place to one side. You can then simply place the bracelet onto the masking tape, line up one end and see if the other end reaches the mark. When doing this remember to allow for the extra length that findings will add to your finished project.

They just keep on rolling

If you are creating a necklace, bracelet or anklet with a range of beads and you are trying to work out the design, find yourself some corduroy. The type with the larger 'grooves' will allow you to place the beads in the grooves in the order you want. This allows you to check if you like your design before you start making your project.

Hair today

If you have a string of fine beads either purchased or in the process of being strung and you need to place it to one side, simply wind around a hair roller (the type you see the ladies wearing in the 50s films when they're having their hair permed). When in place clip the outside holder down and the beads won't become tangled.

Knit one

Try something different and mix wire with knitting. Next time you pass a wool shop pop in and purchase a knitting spool (also known as a Knitting

Nancy). You can then create 'chains' from wire which can be used to create wonderful items of jewelry. When knitting with wire try to use a 28 gauge wire. As your knitting increases in length add a small weight to the bottom, which will help keep the loops on the pegs of the spool and will also help with the tension of your knitting.

Dry as a bone

PMC (Precious Metal Clay) is a great jewelry making material. It allows you to create silver or gold items without the need to be a silver or goldsmith! The best thing about this medium is that if it dries out it can be saved and rehydrated, so nothing goes to waste. To rehydrate place the dry PMC onto a piece of cling film, spray with a fine mist of distilled water, seal the cling film and allow the water to seep into the PMC. Once the PMC has changed color, massage through the cling film. If necessary undo and add a little more water. Allow the clay to sit overnight then massage again. Your clay should now be ready for use.

CRAFTY FACT

It is believed the word 'jewelry' is derived from the word 'jewel' which comes from the old French word 'jouel'. This word can be traced back further to the Latin word 'jocale' meaning plaything. The word bracelet comes from either the Latin word 'brachile' meaning 'of the arm' or from the Old French word 'barcel'.

Smooth as silk

To gain a really smooth finish to your PMC item allow it to dry completely then use a very fine sandpaper to smooth the surface before you fire. Remember to work over plastic wrap, in this way any dust you create can be rehydrated and used again.

"Jewelry making is cheaper than a therapist."

Oily help

When working with PMC if you find it sticks to your hands or work surface then use a few drops of vegetable oil to solve the problem.

Speed drying

Before you fire your PMC item it should be 100% dry. If you can't wait overnight for this process then you can create your own drying box, using a sturdy cardboard box, wire rack, craft knife and hair drier. Simply cut a hole in the side of the box, large enough to hold the hair drier in place. Put the wire rack in the bottom of the box. Leave the front of the box open (for ventilation) and place your items on the rack to dry under the warm air. This should cut down the drying time from overnight to perhaps twenty to thirty minutes.

Hole in one

Remember PMC shrinks as it dries (between 12% to 30% depending on the type) so when making holes for attaching loops etc. make them slightly larger. Otherwise you'll find when you come to attach, the hole you've made may no longer be large enough.

With a little love

Having taken the time to create your new piece of jewelry, you want to care for it so that it lasts. Try not to get it wet as this can weaken the thread you have used. Also chemicals such as perfumes, creams and make-up can lessen the life and impact of your jewelry (especially pearls – both real and imitation), so try to avoid it coming into contact with these. Each time you take off your piece, clean with a soft clean cloth. This will remove any make-up etc. that has got onto your jewelry and stop a build-up.

Storing correctly is also important to ensure the longevity of your jewelry, so ensure on necklaces and bracelets that you close the clasps. In this way they are less likely to become tangled. If the piece is your favorite then you could also wrap it in acid-free tissue paper and store in its own small bag or pouch. And if you intend on selling any of your creations then why not make a small label that you can pop into the bag along with your sale covering these points? Going that little extra always gives a good impression and your customers are more likely to come back if your jewelry lasts and lasts.

Pliers and cutters are the basic kit but what do you use for which job?

Type	Use
Bent nosed pliers	The ends are bent (normally around 90°) and end in a fine point. They are ideal when working on hard to get at places
Chain nosed pliers	The inside of the jaws are flat and the outside are rounded. The jaws come to a point to allow accurate shaping and bending of your wire. They are also very useful when pulling wire and when wire wrapping
Crimp pliers	These allow you to create smooth, rounded crimp beads. As with any new tool they take a little practice but once you've mastered the art you'll never use another pair of pliers to attach those crimps again
Flat nosed pliers	These are your basic pliers with a flat edge on both inside and out. They are suitable for gripping most wires, allowing you to flatten kinks and make angular bends

Type	Use
Flush cutter	These give a smoother cleaner cut than wire cutters. They cut in such a way that when used correctly give you a flat cut on the end left on your project, but a sharp end on the half that is being removed
Nylon pliers	The inside of the pliers are lined with nylon and are ideal when working with very soft wire. They can also be used to harden wire once it has been formed in coils etc. Simply press the wire between the jaws a couple of times and the wire will be harder and more resistant to being misshapen
Round nosed pliers	Great for making simple loops in wire, bending and curving and can be used to turn your leftover wire into cheap jump rings
Side cutter	Ideal for cutting head pins, eye pins and most craft wire
Split right pliers	These are specially designed to open split rings with ease

So the project instructions you're working from provide details of the wire in millimeters or inches but all your wire is labeled in gauges... Then this table is for you:

Wire gauge	Millimeters	Inches
14	1.63	0.064
15	1.45	0.057

Wire gauge	Millimeters	Inches
16	1.29	0.051
17	1.15	0.045
18	1.02	0.040
19	0.91	0.036
20	0.81	0.032
21	0.72	0.029
22	0.64	0.025
23	0.57	0.023
24	0.51	0.020
25	0.45	0.018
26	0.40	0.016
27	0.36	0.014
28	0.32	0.013
29	0.29	0.011
30	0.25	0.010
31	0.23	0.009
32	0.20	0.008

Glass Painting

❝ There are two kinds of people on this planet, those who craft and everyone else! **❞**

Chapter 7
Glass Painting

This craft has recently seen a resurgence with the availability of a huge range of easy-to-use products from water-based paints (which unlike older paints are almost odor free) to purpose-made stickers that allow even the most unsteady hand to have a go at this fun and easy craft. So next time you place that old jam jar in the glass recycle bin, think again; you could be using it to produce something wonderful for your home or creating an unusual gift.

Outline it

When working with outliner, for great results try to allow it to dry completely before beginning the painting process. Overnight is ideal, if you have the time. This has two benefits. Firstly you'll not smudge the outliner if you touch it during the painting process and secondly the outliner will be more effective at holding the pool of paint.

Forever blowing bubbles

The curse of any glass painter is bubbles in the paint. These can be cut down if you do not 'paint' with the brush. That is to say you should drag the paint around with the brush to get it where you want rather than paint in the traditional manner.

It's all fluff

Many glass paints take an age to dry and this gives pet hairs, fluff and dust more opportunities to land on your project. To reduce the chances of your work being ruined, place the project in a large box that can be closed and put out of the way. This will also cut down on the possibility of curious fingers wanting to touch the project to see if it is dry!

Alright with white

When using white paint with dark outliners (bronze or traditional black) the paint can stain the outliner. So if possible try to paint on the reverse of the piece. In this way the outliner will not become stained, thereby improving the finish.

Outliner alternatives

When in a rush or you just don't want to use the traditional method of outlining there are 'cheat' alternatives that work well. The first are stickers that are simply stuck onto the glass then painted as normal. You can also use rubber stamps on glass and heat emboss, which creates an almost instant outline.

CRAFTY FACT

The earliest proof of glassblowing was found in the form of 'waste' glass tubes, rods and tiny blown bottles found in Jerusalem that are believed to date between 37 BC and 4 BC.

Stamp it out

When stamping and embossing on glass there are a couple of things to remember. Firstly, don't let the heat gun touch the glass as this can crack the glass. Secondly, do a test with the embossing powder and the paint you are using. Sometimes the paints react with the embossing powder and will lift it from the glass. If this occurs you have a couple of choices. Perhaps paint the project on the reverse, so the paint does not come into contact with the embossed image. Alternatively change the embossing powder or paints you are using and repeat the testing process until you find a combination that works.

Bother with bubbles

Most outliners come in tubes which have to be squeezed to apply, very similar to piping icing onto a cake. Unfortunately sometimes air can get trapped in the nozzle which can then create problems when you are working. To help overcome this problem always squeeze a little outliner onto a tissue to check there are no air bubbles before you start. Also as you work, keep wiping the tip of the tube on the tissue; this should also help prevent lines becoming too thick.

Clean before you start

Even when working on a glass item that has been purchased just for the purpose of decorating you should always make sure it is 100% clean. To do this wash in warm soapy water and allow to dry naturally or clean using a product such as white spirit or methylated spirit.

Not just for glass

Glass paints are not just for glass. Perhaps paint onto acetate then create a unique card. You could then match the card to a glass painted gift. Glass paints also work extremely well on aluminum cans and kitchen tin foil, giving another dimension to your painting.

Bead-dazzled

Try adding extra interest to your painting in the form of seed beads. Simply drop the beads where you want them using a pair of tweezers whilst the paint is still wet. The wet paint will act like glue and when dry the beads will be stuck in place.

All that glitters

Fine glitters can also be added to paints, so you can add a real shimmer to your designs. Simply sprinkle the glitter over your project whilst the paint is still wet then allow to dry. If you only want the glitter in one place, ensure the other areas of paint are 100% dry before you sprinkle the glitter onto the wet area.

Cover those faults

If you find a stray piece of fluff or pet hair has landed on your work or you missed that dreaded bubble, as long as the paint is tacky there is a remedy. Take a stiff clean brush and bounce the ends of the brush up and down on the surface of the paint. This will break up the paint's surface and give it a texture; this texture will hide any flaw and when asked the technique is called stippling!

Transferring a design

One of the great things about glass painting is you don't actually have to be able to draw to produce works of art. Many designs can either be traced through to the glass or traced onto the glass. However working with bottles and jars can be difficult as you have to hold the pattern in place whilst you are working. One method that allows you to hold the design right up against the glass and ensures the design does not get distorted, is to place the design inside the jars then fill with grains of rice or something similar.

❝ Me an addict? I only glass paint on days that end in Y, so where's the problem? **❞**

Having a 'reel' good time

When working in the round it is difficult to know where to hold the project without smudging your outliner. So next time a reel of adhesive tape or masking tape runs out don't throw it away, it's a great aid for your glass painting. It can be used to hold jars and other similar items whilst you work. Outline one side, working as far round as you can then allow the outliner to fully dry. Then turn the project and work on the next section.

Mirror, mirror on the wall

When creating a design on a mirror you obviously cannot place the design behind the glass to trace it through. You therefore need to transfer the design in another way. Old fashioned carbon paper is ideal for this. You simply place the carbon paper onto the mirror, place your design over this then trace your design. If you use a different colored pen from the one the design was originally drawn with then you'll see any bits you've missed as you work.

Oh smudge!

When working with liquid outliner it can sometimes get smudged or go where you don't want it to. Thankfully there are two methods for overcoming this problem. The first is to use a damp Q-Tip which you twist as you wipe over the smudge. As you work, try to ensure you don't touch a good area. The second method is to dry the outliner with a hair drier then use the tip of a craft knife to scrape off just the line that needs to be removed.

Inspire me

Sometimes your muse will let you down, so you will have to go looking for inspiration. Search out children's coloring books, wrapping paper, greeting cards, posters, magazines, catalogs and craft books including glass painting books. Or try the internet which is a great place to look. Simply search using the term 'free glass painting designs' and you'll be amazed just how many come up.

Diamonds are a girl's best friend

To add a little 3-D decoration to your design give flat backed glass jewels (often called glass nuggets) a try. They come in a huge range of colors or you could use clear ones and paint them to match your design. To attach securely use a good quality two-part resin, often know as epoxy resin.

Big is best

To cut down on the chances of bubbles when working on a large area use a pipette to apply the paint instead of a brush. Simply place the pipette in the middle of the outlined area then slowly add the color and allow the paint to flow until the area is full.

Fade from light to dark

When painting try to start with light colors first then work through to dark. This will cut down on the possibility of colors contaminating one another. Also as you work clean your brush between colors to keep your color clean.

Straight there

To create a straight line when outlining touch the nozzle onto the glass surface then apply a gentle, even pressure. Then lift the nozzle away from the surface and stretch the outliner along in a straight line. Touch the nozzle down on the glass surface at the end of your line to finish.

Sponge it!

If you wish to cover a large area and would like a texture, then sponging is a good way of applying paint. See sensational stencils tip below!

Finishing touch

Some manufacturers produce a varnish that comes in a gloss or matt finish which gives added protection to your work. So if you know your project is likely to be handled a lot then search out a suitable varnish.

Sensational stencils

Sometimes you can work the other way round from the traditional 'outliner then painting' method by applying the paint first. This can be used to great effect with stencils. Spray the back of the stencil with a little repositionable spray glue and attach to your glass. Use a fine sponge and apply the paint, remove the stencil then allow the paint to dry. You can then add detail by using outliner over the top of the paint.

Top to toe

When working on a new project try to start at the top and work down. In this way you'll not smudge outliner or paint with the side of your hand as you work.

Something a little different

Why not experiment? Perhaps apply a dark color over a light color whilst the first is still wet. Or allow the first coat to dry then paint detail over the top in a second darker color. If you have solvent paint many will allow you to marble (just in the way paper is marbled).

CRAFTY FACT

Early glass was always coloured with a faint hint of green or brown, this was because of impurities. It was not until the 1st century that clear glass was discovered. The 15th century Venetian glass makers used manganese to make fine colorless, transparent glass.

" Just remind them, a house becomes a home when you can write 'I love you' on the furniture. **"**

Useful Websites

www.thecraftark.com

Over 500 free craft projects, many with step-by-step photographs, instructional video and sign-up for free newsletter.

www.craftplace.org

Free projects and crafting tips, has a good section for teachers looking for ideas and help in the classroom.

www.craftfreebies.com

Includes hundreds of free craft patterns, free craft projects and craft ideas.

www.diynetwork.com/topics/crafting

A good range of craft ideas and projects from beading to scrapbooking.

www.makingmemories.com

Primarily for the 'Scrapbooker' but includes lots of ideas that can also be used to create cards and paper related projects.

www.freecraftz.com

Free craft patterns and free craft templates.

www.northpolechristmas.com

Free craft patterns for the Christmas season with complete instructions.

www.sewing.org

Instructions for sewing and a whole bunch of sewing projects; ideal if you want to sew for charity.

www.ilovetocraft.com

A whole range of free craft projects with a kids' section to get them crafting as well.

www.craftcreations.com

A crafting store with free craft project magazines you can download.

www.craftsolutions.com

A directory of craft ideas, craft projects, websites and more.

www.allfreecrafts.com

Ideas and patterns plus a range of free eBooks you can download.

www.craftzine.com

Craft projects and podcasts.

Index